A BIT MORE BOATING

Shirley Ginger

Lucifer Press

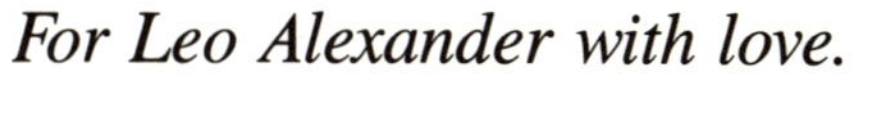

For Leo Alexander with love.

First published in Great Britain by
Lucifer Press
Foxwhelp · Mathon · Near Malvern
Worcestershire WR13 5PW

A catalogue record of this title is held at the British Library

ISBN 0 9519198 1 4

Typeset and printed in Great Britain by
Woodfield Publishing Services
Fontwell · West Sussex · England

CONTENTS

O denotes Norton Junction, the hub of the book

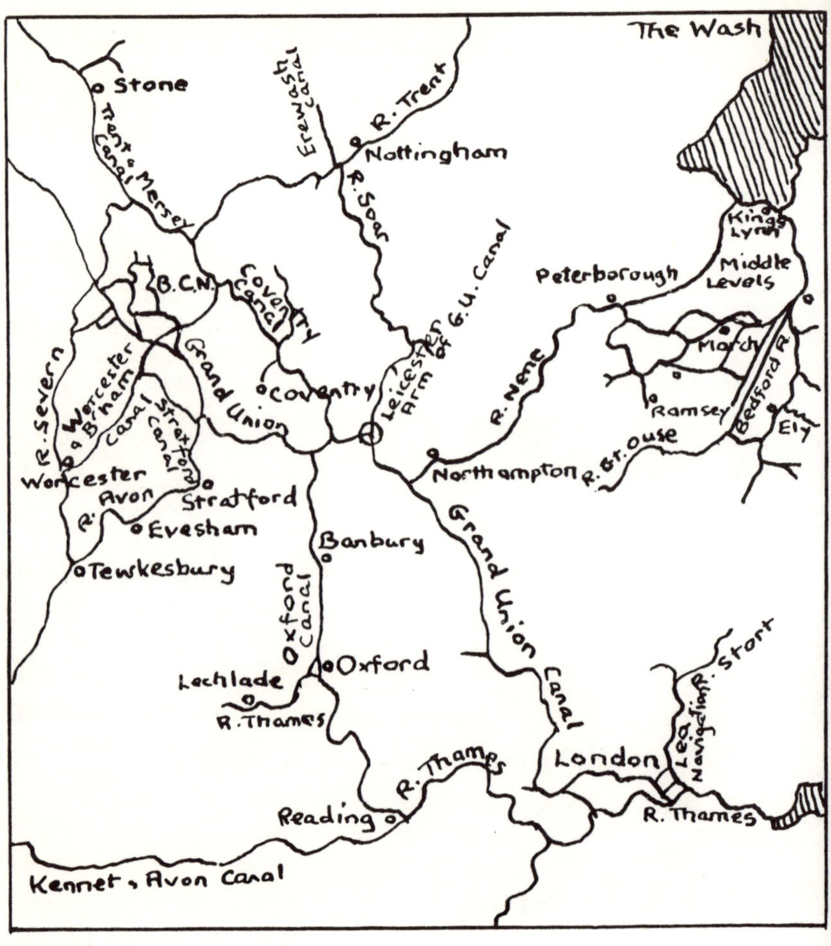

Simple view of places and waterways mentioned in the following pages

= 1 =

TUNNEL VISION

"I declare this tunnel well and truly open!"

At least, that is what I thought Sir Leslie Young said when he cut the tape to allow the first boat through on that red-letter day but the cheers were so deafening as they echoed off the steep sides of the cutting and my own excitement so intense that I could not be sure. Of all the traders on the Grand Union Canal, I doubt any had felt the partition of north from south more acutely than my husband Maurice and myself. For four years we had struggled to make a living from a smallholding and general stores catering almost exclusively for the needs of boaters. Blisworth Tunnel, all 3,065 yards of it, was barely fifteen miles from us and during its long closure had deprived us (we were convinced) of the free-spending rich boaters from London and the south-east.

But all that was now history, I thought as I squelched through the mud oozing down from the rain-sodden fields and made my way towards the northern portal. The sun burned in a clear sky and trees steamed as crowds gathered and boats assembled. Everyone was far too early and what had started as an orderly procession of miscellaneous craft – from scruffy little inflatables to immaculate immense Joshers – degenerated into a shambles as people tried to jump the queue. I had no idea how many boats were waiting at the Stoke Bruerne end of the tunnel, which would not officially be opened until Sir Leslie had passed through, but there must have been fifty or sixty at my end and tempers were beginning to fray as fervour mounted. Our own boat, Warwickshire Lad, had been brought along to the ceremony by our daughter Stephanie but sensibly she took one look at the mayhem and decided to moor well out of harm's way. Then she joined me on the bank by the tunnel entrance to witness the spectacle and report it later on Independent Radio News.

After a bit, there was a lot of hooting and a buzz went through the crowd. Sir Leslie and a load of bigwigs aboard the trip-boat Saucy Sue hove into sight round the bend. A cheer went up and somehow the tangle of boats, with much shoving and waving of shafts, unravelled itself and allowed Saucy Sue to approach the tunnelmouth first.

Snip- it was done!

Snip – it was done! Saucy Sue disappeared into the blackness closely followed by the eager convoy. I said cheerio to Stephanie and retraced my muddy footsteps to the boatyard where Dianne Gill had kindly allowed me a cranny in the car park for my aged Volkswagen Beetle. She pressed me to stay for a celebration party but I guessed that Maurice would be trying to cope with an unusual amount of trade back in the shop at Buckby Top Lock and would be desperate for another pair of hands. I was glad, though, to be told later that when the furore had died down Warwickshire Lad cruised through the tunnel and so earned a special commemorative plaque. It had been such an important event for all of us.

After driving briskly home along the leafy lanes of Northamptonshire to Buckby Wharf, I was surprised to find that Maurice was not as busy as expected. In fact, the afternoon was much the same as any sunny Wednesday in August might have been. There was the usual flow of hire boats from the north carrying people who had never heard of tunnel closures and were puzzled by the single topic of conversation which kept cropping up everywhere. We warned a few of the novices who came in to the shop that they might expect a traffic jam as they approached Blisworth but I doubt if they took us seriously. No one changed their planned route on the strength of our advice but several people popped in to see us on their way back and said how much they wished they had!

Nobody – not the British Waterways Board, who obligingly brought forward the date of the tunnel reopening so that southern boat owners could more easily get to Coventry by Friday; not the Inland Waterways Association who had organised the National Rally of Boats at Hawkesbury Junction due to take place over the coming Bank Holiday weekend; not the local canalside traders or Midlands hire firms and certainly not the unsuspecting holidaymakers who had hired their boats in the sublime faith that they were getting a stress-free country cruise – anticipated the fury that some boaters could unleash when they were thwarted.

Trouble began at six-thirty sharp. Looking back, it is easy to see why and amazing that it was not foreseen by anyone in authority.

The nearest hire firm to the south of us was about halfway between the bottom of the Buckby flight of seven locks and Blisworth tunnel. They offered hire periods starting on different days; a sensible arrangement which normally helped to ease congestion at locks. But today was far from normal. Only one of their boats arrived at Buckby Bottom Lock in time.

In time for what? Well that particular year was one of exceptionally low rainfall. It has been common enough since and now we all know about climatic changes we are not too surprised. But this was the first dry one of any significance since the drought of '76. There were notices everywhere asking boaters to conserve water. It was spelt out; share locks, if necessary waiting for other craft to catch you up. Not such a penance – it is a great way of making new friends. We still keep in touch with a Manchester family we first met in a lock on the Trent and

Mersey fourteen years ago! It also halves the effort. And it does not take a minute to peer under a bridge or round a corner to make sure there is no boat coming the other way before you change the lock's water level in your own favour. 'Waiting turns' it is called and has sometimes been compulsory. Now, it is reasonable and good manners. And there was little of either about, British Waterways bosses decided. So knowing about the rally and the tunnel, they guessed that the Buckby flight of locks was one on which restrictions would have to be imposed, willy-nilly, if what is known as the Braunston summit were not to dry up altogether. The lock-keeper was instructed to put padlocks on the gates of both top and bottom locks at 6.30 p.m. precisely and leave them on all night. And that is what the poor man did.

At the precise moment that he was snapping the padlock shut, a boat slammed into the coping stones below the bottom lock and the irate captain charged up the steps brandishing a windlass and yelling with rage at the sight of the hire boat he could see rising in the lock above him. He hadn't come through the bloody tunnel first, he raged, to stay at the bottom of Buckby and lose any decent mooring there might be had at the rally. Another boat arrived and its owner sprinted up, unarmed. He dissuaded the other chap from using violence and tried a honey tongue instead. Neither worked. The lock-keeper hopped on his bicycle and whizzed as fast as he could pedal to the top where he let out those boats which had lawfully entered the flight before 6.30. He went back down later, with a mate, to do the reverse, and on his return told us of the line of boats tied up as far as the eye could see and of the anger seething among the frustrated crews gathered at the foot of the flight.

"There must be seventy boats," he said, whey-faced, "and more coming, from what I've heard."

Wow!" I said to Maurice in trepidation. "What are we in for tomorrow?"

"Trouble," said he, adding practically, "unless I quadruple our order for bread and milk."

"It's like the olden days," I reflected, "when there were fisticuffs on the staircase locks at Watford."

"Hm," grunted Maurice. "There's one major difference these fellows seem to have forgotten. They're not working for a living on their boats – they're on holiday."

"And what's more – they're supposed to be celebrating," I said sadly.

We were up early the next morning, woken by the baker who arrived at first light. Our usual practice was to ring him during the evening and give him our order for the following day. He would then leave the bread in an outside storeroom for us to take in at a more civilised hour. Today, he'd hit a snag, he said. We groaned. What now?

"A lightning strike – unofficial," he said, "so I'm short of bread. I can only let you have half your order."

"Couldn't you have warned us?" I asked, thinking about irate skippers waving windlasses over my head for our last bap.

"Didn't know myself," he said. "You're not the only ones to be let down."

"I suppose not," I replied, certain that Long Buckby housewives were likely to be more reasonable about the shortfall than some of our customers.

"I'll have to drive into Northampton," said Maurice, carrying the trays of bread inside. "We can't afford to run out of bread today."

I agreed wholeheartedly. "Get a couple of cases of long-life milk at the same time, just in case the cows are on strike too!"

The lock-keeper unlocked the flight betimes. "They've simmered down," he reported to me on his return. "But give me an ounce of St.Bruno to be going on with – I think I'm going to need it."

"Would that be 25 grammes?" I asked, "I can never remember."

"That's right, me duck." He paused in the shop doorway to fill his pipe. "I suppose it's unkind to ask for rain on a Bank Holiday weekend – but sure as shooting I wish it would!"

I smiled, torn between wanting rain for the garden and the reservoirs and sunshine to boost trade. Good weather always had that effect, even if it was only lager, ice-cream and soft drinks.

I heard the crunch of tyres on the gravel shortly after the lock-keeper had crossed over to his own cottage for breakfast.

It was Maurice back. "Everything O.K.?" he asked.

"Only boats going down, so far," I said. "Oh, good – you got some extra ice-cream as well. I'll put it in our own freezer outside as a reserve."

"Forecast's for the heat wave to last over the weekend." He always listened to the radio avidly in the car – it was the only chance he ever had. "There was another piece from Stephanie about the tunnel. Boats still flooding up from London, she says."

"Where was Warwickshire Lad when she made the broadcast?"

"Milton Keynes."

"I hope they're back tomorrow," I said. "She promised to help me with our stand at the rally on Saturday."

"There's always Bruce." He reminded me that our son was coming home for the weekend with Becky. They lived in Oxford.

"I've earmarked them for Sunday," I said.

Just then we heard the ring of pawls as the paddles on the lower gates of our lock were raised.

"Here we go!" said Maurice.

From then on we never stopped. The lock-keeper made everybody share locks whether they liked it or not – and owners of fibreglass cruisers often resist sharing with steel boats. Sometimes there were as many as four boats in the lock at the same time. And the occupants all wanted to do their holiday shopping while the lock filled so that they would not be delayed one second more than it needed for some 60,000 gallons of water to flow in through the sluices. This generally took about fifteen minutes. But a quarter of an hour was not enough for so many people to do their shopping when umpteen children were clamouring for ice-cream at the same time. Good manners flew out of the window – we tried to retain ours but it got very difficult. Occasionally, someone would explain that they wanted to be out of the shop as soon as the lock gates opened. As if we did not know!

"So does everybody," I said firmly, "and this gentleman (nodding towards an inoffensive lorry driver who had been pushed to the back twice) was here first."

By three o'clock, we were not only exhausted but starving, having not eaten since a sketchy breakfast at seven.

"Food," implored Maurice, "before I collapse. We'll shut for twenty minutes and have a breather." He vaulted the counter and turned the little wooden sign to 'Closed'. A howl of rage came from the half full lock. "Twenty minutes," he called. "That's all. You can tie up here."

They did not, of course.

We gulped a quick meal. The microwave came into its own at times like this. I made vast casseroles before the season started and froze them in individual portions ready to be taken out, thawed, and swallowed on the run. Often we took it in turns to eat – it was rare to shut the shop for lunch. But today we needed the break to recover our equilibrium.

"There!" said Maurice with satisfaction. "I can smile now."

It was just as well because the next person to walk in the door was a young woman from a hired boat travelling south. Tears were running down her cheeks and she put her windlass down on the counter with trembling fingers.

"Have you any paracetamol?" She sniffed. "I think I'm getting a migraine."

"Of course" I said sympathetically.

"Is it always like this?"

"There are fewer boats around as a rule. Has something happened to upset you?"

"We were in that tunnel back there..."

"Braunston?"

"Yes – that's it. Our first tunnel." She gulped. "And suddenly we saw two boats in front coming towards us. You've no idea how frightened we were – they were simply enormous and side by side, tied together I think. They hooted and hooted and then there was a lot of shouting before they hit us. They told my husband to go backwards but he couldn't steer properly in reverse and we kept bumping into the side. It was awful. The people at the boatyard told us we could pass in the tunnel – they didn't say anything about giving way to working boats."

"What working boats?" I said dryly. "None have been through here today. They were just as much on holiday as you are and they'd no right to go through breasted up."

"Well, they've spoilt my holiday anyway," she said. "We've an even longer tunnel to go through tomorrow and then both of them again coming back. I dread it."

"Don't worry," I said more optimistically than I felt, "I don't suppose it'll happen again."

One of the next pair of boats to rise up in the lock was Ben, an unconverted old seventy-footer. It belonged to the Lloyds. Shaun was secretary of the Narrow Boat Owners Club. Just the man to deal with this problem, I thought, as his huge bulk darkened the shop doorway. I told him about the incident.

"Shocking," he agreed, "and designed to put a first-timer off boating for good. But they weren't our members, I'll vouch for that. It'll be the London mob! Leaving both the top gates open as usual – I've been cursing them all the way up the flight."

"Ah, yes." I knew all about that. It seems to be a tradition south of Leighton Buzzard to ignore British Waterways orders to close lock gates after yourself on the grounds that 'we don't do that in London'. It can be very irritating when you arrive at a wide lock and invariably find that you have to go to the opposite end and shut the gates before you start to do anything else. It also allows precious water to leak away. Last time we cruised to London we counted fifteen B.W. notices on separate locks and still the gates were wide open!

"Anyway," said Shaun, "we're right behind them. I'll sort 'em out when I catch up with them." He grinned and gave me a wave as he heaved himself aboard Ben. I did not envy the cowboys!

= 2 =

RALLY REFLECTIONS

Saturday promised to be a scorcher. The National Rally of Boats was due to open to the public at 10.30 a.m. and I allowed ourselves a couple of hours in which to get to Hawkesbury Junction on the outskirts of Coventry and set up our display. I had been painting canal ware like fury in the halcyon days before the tunnel reopened and we had a splendid stock of Buckby cans in all sizes from miniature mantelpiece ornaments to practical five gallon vessels suitable for a seventy foot long narrow boat. They were originally used to carry drinking water but now, except on a few boats whose owners had chosen not to modernise by installing a freshwater tank, were mainly for decoration. And very decorative they are, with roses and castles in cheerful colours. We also had other traditional items; a horse's nose bowl complete with leather strap to hang round his neck, corn scoops in different colours, coke hods, buckets and dippers, all smothered in roses. Then there were 20th century gifts painted in the same manner; pots, brushes, mugs and plates – even tobacco tins. We also took along tee and sweat shirts printed with my design showing a wide lock beneath rain clouds captioned 'summer and winter on the Grand Union Canal' (hardly appropriate that particular weekend), sticks of Buckby Wharf rock, packets of fudge, notelets and postcards. The stand looked very jolly and colourful and the storage space under the table was screened with waterways tea towels.

Stephanie and I were easily ready by 10.30 a.m. and waited eagerly for the customers to come surging into the marquee. Nothing happened. Coventry, it seemed, was doing its weekend shopping in the city centre. The few people wandering past were other exhibitors..

"Don't worry," said our left hand neighbour, Bill Hickey, a regular at boat rallies. "It'll be busier after lunch – it always is."

He was a Thames lighterman and made rope fenders in his spare time.

"He can't relax," said his wife said cheerfully, "unless he's twiddling string in his hands, inventing ways of tying knots."

Bill had an array of fenders in all shapes and sizes and colours of rope. He showed me the handsome leather box in which he kept the tools he used – each one nestling in its allotted place. Then, because I expressed interest, the next day he brought me the tome he had acquired in the merchant navy and which described the skill of fender-making in great detail accompanied by fine pen and ink drawings.

On our right was a second hand book stall which was irresistible to Stephanie. She browsed and bought a slim, fusty volume which kept her occupied until the tent began to fill up, as Bill had forecast, after lunch.

Opposite us, John Hill of Fishley was showing some of his painted ware. Secretly, I thought this was a pity although I like John. He paints well and had been doing it longer than me. The very first watercan we bought for Warwickshire Lad was painted by him. It is an Aylesbury can with a wooden handle and we still have it. Unfortunately it is not galvanised and has gone rusty on the inside so is unsuitable for drinking water. Although we have a proper modern water tank on our boat, the pump has been known to pack up in which case a watercan comes in handy! We always travel with a full one now. It also makes it more difficult to steal a big can off the roof if it is heavy. They look very tempting, I always think, to an unscrupulous passer-by.

We first met John Hill when we were all members of the Birmingham Canal Navigation Society years ago. I took my turn at manning the society stand when the Boat Show used to be at Bingley Hall in Birmingham (on the site of the new conference centre) and John supplied the B.C.N.S. with painted ware to sell. Maybe he still does. A lot of the fun of the waterways fraternity is that no matter where you are on the system, you are bound to meet someone you know.

Stephanie and I took it in turns to have a walk round everything the rally had to offer. The prime moorings were occupied by floating exhibits, mostly provided by boatbuilders and hire fleet operators. Neither interested me much so I eschewed them but Stephanie took a look and came back full of the shortcomings of dear old Warwickshire Lad.

"What do we want with central heating?" I asked her. "We've got an efficient multifuel stove in the middle of our thirty-five feet.

You can't get more central than that! And the fuel's often free." Maurice never let a piece of wood float past without fishing it out for the fire.

There were about seven hundred other boats moored for a mile up each of the three canals which met at the junction. As I had seen enough of these the previous Thursday, I did not bother with them either. I could hear the fun fair warming up on the other side of the old engine house. It would not get into full swing until after Sir Leslie performed the official opening ceremony at 2.30 p.m. The main trade show, of which we were part, included a licensed bar, a breakfast and lunch tent, a continuous pig roast, a permanent barbecue and over fifty trade stands, a number of which were more in keeping with a car boot sale than a gathering of boats.

I strolled out of the field gateway and past the Greyhound Pub which had been given a face lift for the occasion. It was not the only thing at Hawkesbury to have been smartened up, I thought, looking at superficially restored old buildings, tastefully designed new ones, shiny paint on the graceful cast-iron bridge, blue and red brick edgings to cinder paths and extensive planting of 'civic' trees. What a lot it must have cost! And yet this was traditionally a fund-raising event by the Inland Waterways Association which campaigned for the continuation and improvement of navigable and disused waterways. Or so I had always thought. But this rally was being sponsored by their old adversary, the British Waterways Board. The site at Hawkesbury, like Tipton, was planned as one of the permanent venues for boat rallies. Which left me wondering about neglected waterways never to be favoured with 'venue' status.

I cast my mind back to the first National Rally to which we had taken Warwickshire Lad. It had been exactly ten years before, at Nottingham. My clearest recollection is one of fun. The site was the river Trent, which being a wide waterway swallowed up the six hundred or so boats without anyone having to walk very far to the hub of things. We had not booked a place in advance and were allotted a mooring alongside a number of boats belonging to members of the Lymm Cruising Club who readily absorbed us into their jollifications. In the nearby field were a handful of trade stands, one of which was Ladyline, sponsor of the rally. The majority of stalls belonged to various canal societies raising money for their particular waterway.

The aims of the rally, the brochure told us, were to raise funds for the National Waterways Restoration Fund, encourage greater commercial use of the Trent and support the Grantham Canal Restoration Fund. A miniature narrow boat named Baby Grumplin advertised the latter. The entertainment was mostly a conglomeration of good amateurs: comedians, unamplified music and sketches – all waterway orientated and some of it impromptu. A monologue about Uncle Joe's Mint Balls had young Bruce doubled up with glee until he fell off his chair!

As we had not originally planned to attend the Nottingham rally, we left on the morning of the Bank Holiday to continue our summer cruise which was to take us back up the Trent and Cranfleet Cut. When we got to the broad intersection where the Soar Navigation enters from the south almost opposite Trent Lock, the big sailing club at the junction was holding a regatta. The myriad multicoloured sails, dipping and whirling, would have been an engaging sight had we not known that engine gives way to sail. As it was, we concentrated on doing our best to take evasive action but no doubt made a few enemies before we reached the haven of the lock and the entrance to the Erewash canal.

This was a second diversion. The reason was that we had been infected with the enthusiasm of members of the Erewash Canal Preservation and Development Association. 'Hardly anyone boats right to the head of navigation', they had told us plaintively in Nottingham. 'It's such a shame after all the effort we've put into the restoration of the canal'. 'O.K.,' we said obligingly, not realising what we were in for but tempted by the idea of a rewarding certificate at the end of it. So up through the lock we went accompanied by Warlock, a much longer boat than ours and drawing several inches more which was encouraging. Warlock stopped almost straight away at a boatyard, the steerer wishing us the best of luck. This should have rung warning bells in our heads. But we had only been boat owners for a year or two and were still wet behind the ears.

Above the lock, a long line of houseboats lurked beneath the overhanging willows. 'Slow Down' said a large red notice, fiercely repeated several times. Dutifully, we did; losing way and grinding crablike through the silt on the towpath side. I glared at the houseboats which did not stir within their mats of waterlilies. There was a strong suspicion in my mind that they were comfortably sitting on the mud and not floating at all.

So up through the lock we went

It took us two hours to get to Sandiacre, a matter of only three miles but the lock gear was stiff and the chambers of all three locks slow to empty and fill. We tied up in the rain at the municipal wharf with its clipped lawn and cherry trees and had supper. Then, determined to get to the head of navigation, on we went.

In those days, Stanton Ironworks was still in business and we blamed it for our problems which began below Stanton lock. First of all, the propeller was seized with weed – not an uncommon occurrence in summer on a little used waterway. We had an easily accessible weedhatch, so Maurice cleared it without difficulty. It seized again… and again… and again, until eventually we entered the lock. The paddle gear was even worse than on the previous locks and although Bruce had a good set of muscles for a twelve year old he allowed the windlass to slip off the spindle. It whizzed round and flew off, striking him on the side of his head so that his ears sang and a lump the size of a ping-pong ball erupted. Eventually we had the lock filled and the top gates partially open. It was a good thing the locks were broad ones as neither gate would open more than halfway because of the rubbish behind it. However, there was room enough for us, so out we thought we would go.

Not likely! The weed (duck variety) was so dense that irrespective of propeller and engine, Warwickshire Lad would not budge. All four of us tried to haul the boat forward by the ropes but it was hopeless. A fly stuck in treacle would have had as much chance of breaking free.

"We'll have to stay here this evening," said Maurice. It was a quarter past eight.

"Then what?" I asked.

"Reverse out tomorrow and try and turn round at the top of the last lock." The children moaned disappointedly.

"We won't get a certificate," said Stephanie.

"It's far too noisy here," I grumbled. "I bet that place works all night." As if in response, a hooter sounded, making us all flinch.

"Well, what do you suggest?" Maurice often did that – put the ball in my court and mentally sauntered off to indicate that I could not possibly hit it back. This time I did.

"We'll ask the iron workers to pull us clear," I announced, observing a dozen men running down a metal staircase from a doorway and heading in our direction. "That hooter must've signalled the end of a shift." I approached the first chap and asked him nicely. Amiably, he summoned his mates.

Ten minutes and twenty four biceps later we were on our way. The cause of the duckweed was soon plain. Canal water flowed into the cooling system of the steel works via a spillway covered in steel mesh. The build up of rubbish against the filter trapped the weed which flourished in the warmed water. It only ever flowed downhill when the lock was used and this was rarely. We stopped and pulled some of the larger pieces of timber and plastic bags off the mesh and on our way back were untroubled by the weed.

It had rained heavily the previous night, causing water to pour over the bottom gates of the locks but this did nothing to increase the depth of the canal. We dragged our way to Eastwood and tied up in steaming sunshine. *The Rainbow* was one of my Open University set books that year so I persuaded Maurice to toil up the steep hill to the town with me in search of the birthplace of D.H.Lawrence. It was in a row of brick terrace houses and next door to a hairdresser called 'Shirley' which I considered a good omen for my forthcoming examination. Lawrence's house was empty and neglected. The only indication of its authenticity was a small engraved plate above the door. We peered in through curtainless windows at scraps of flowered wallpaper and a steep narrow staircase beside the hearth. The house was only one tiny room deep and the back door gave on to a yard with a privy and lean-to. I marvelled that genius could emerge from such roots. I believe the house is a museum now, but I prefer to remember it as I saw it then.

We walked back across the fields in search of the disused Nottingham Canal which runs alongside the Erewash for a large part of its length. It was easy to find because a path from Eastwood crosses it by a footbridge close to the remains of a lock. The canal was clothed in grass and stubby hawthorn bushes. Reeds grew in the soft mud at the bottom indicating a source of water still trickling along it.

Bruce and Stephanie were impatiently waiting on the boat when we got back, anxious that we should not arrive at Langley Mill after the lock-keeper had gone off duty.

"How will we get our certificate if he's not there?" asked Stephanie worriedly.

"We'll get it," said Bruce, the optimist.

Langley Mill Lock came as a surprise as it was not marked on the chart, probably because it had been recently restored. It lifted us into the Great Northern Basin created originally by the junction of the Erewash, Nottingham and Cromford Canal, which is mostly derelict. The children scampered gleefully over to the lock cottage where Leslie Allsopp signed a facsimile of the old Erewash Canal Company's bylaws – our certificate.

Recently, Maurice and I travelled up the Erewash Canal on our own. We saw only one other boat on the move. Dredgers had been at work on the channel which was wider and marginally deeper than in '74. The locks seemed just as tough going! There had been much building of housing and industrial estates; making the surroundings less rural than I remembered. We got ourselves another certificate, for old times' sake. Signed, not by Mr Allsopp who has retired but the chairman of the canal society. He was cock-a-hoop because that very day he had learnt of their success in the fight to prevent open-cast mining in the valley of the river Erewash. A triumph indeed!

We do not take Warwickshire Lad to boat rallies anymore. In fact, we tend to go in the opposite direction if it is convenient. There is so much pressure on water supplies and queues at flights of locks that we feel it takes a lot of the joy out of boating. Sometimes we attend by car for one reason or another.

Milton Keynes followed Hawkesbury as a site for the National Rally. The entertainments were even more spectacular and less waterway orientated. As well as the fun fair, which had become a regular event, they included American football and a motor cycle display! We went along for two reasons. One was to buy a set of Bill Hickey's excellent side fenders and the other was to judge the Illuminated Boat Competition. I had been invited to do this by the social secretary of the Milton Keynes branch of the Inland Waterways Association. Libby suggested that we viewed the procession from the roof of her beautiful boat, Pendragon, and her husband plied me with home-made wine while we waited. It is a miracle that I was not illuminated myself by the time I had to do the judging and just as well that Maurice drove us home afterwards! I found it very difficult to choose; everyone had put in such a lot of effort and there were several ingenious and original ideas. I fell in love with an iridescent mermaid on the roof of Ada Florence and chose her. Maurice and Stephanie disagreed with me because they said that mermaids live in the sea but I overruled them with a rare feeling of power. Anyway – how can they be so sure?

= 3 =

CHICKEN FEED

Summer lingered reluctantly into September. Strong winds and dark skies had seen August out, to be succeeded by warm, muggy weather. The sun, when it burst through purple cloud, was bright and hot. But no rain fell. Watering the garden every night after we had closed the shop was a lengthy chore. A sprinkler has its uses but a lot of moisture is lost by evaporation before it hits the soil, even in the late evening. Young trees and shrubs, of which we had many, needed a bucketful apiece and so did the marrows and courgettes. Runner beans want a thorough soaking too; a sprinkling of water is worse than none at all as it draws the roots up to the surface. Our policy of self-sufficiency makes us acutely conscious of the weather.

Lack of rain is bad news for almost everything, not just plants. Hens, for example, drink more water than most people realise. A dozen birds will shift about a gallon daily when they are in lay. Free range hens graze widely and drink less when the grass is sappy but now it looked dry and parched. I mention hens in particular because I had become carried away by my recent successes at rearing poultry.

Our original hens had been commercially bred Warrens which are hybrids. Normally, these do not go broody although one of ours did. Sadly, a fox took her. The pullets she had reared died of fright in the same incident but the young cockerel survived and was now at the peak of his powers. If we wanted a plentiful supply of eggs to sell the following season, now was the time to get a new generation going. As the likelihood of another broody hen materialising seemed remote, Maurice had snapped up a second-hand incubator from a lad who had become bored with raising exotic birds.

Neither of us had the least idea how incubators worked but we assumed it was commonsense. I did not have doubts until Maurice had unpacked the box and I read the brief instructions and the ominous list of potential problems.

"Sticky navel!" I exclaimed. "That sounds horrible. D'you suppose it's fatal?"

"Haven't the foggiest," said Maurice. "I didn't know chicks had navels. Let's see if the incubator works first." The indicator light glowed satisfactorily, so I set about following the instructions carefully. First I wiped the circular polystyrene base and clear plastic top with disinfectant and scrubbed the wire interior tray thoroughly. I also disinfected the tiny thermometer and humidifier. There were three vital factors for a successful hatching, I learnt, apart from the quality of the eggs which must be fresh and perfectly shaped: a damp atmosphere, frequent turning of the eggs and a constant temperature of 101° Fahrenheit. It was the third requirement which caused us the biggest problem and it was several days before the temperature in the incubator had stopped fluctuating enough to risk putting a dozen eggs inside. I expected heat to be lost when I opened it to turn the eggs every few hours but sometimes it hotted up for no apparent reason. On the fourteenth day, the thermometer shot up to 104° several times.

"The chicks will be cooked!" I said to Maurice. "What's the matter with it?"

"Turn the thermostat down," he said. I did, then it cooled too much and I had to turn it up again. We moved the incubator into the bedroom so that we could check the temperature in the night and decided to leave it there until the eggs hatched – if they ever did.

On the nineteenth day, I stopped turning the eggs as instructed. The next morning I noticed a tiny bulge in the shell of one of the eggs. In between customers, I kept running upstairs to see what was happening. There were hairline cracks radiating from the bulge the next time I looked, and another egg had a single big crack. I could hear a faint scuffling and chipping from inside the incubator.

"Some of them have survived, anyway," I said to Maurice excitedly.

By five o'clock, six eggs had pipped and the tips of minute beaks could be seen pecking away at the holes. There was also a piercing intermittent tweeting. The first chick hatched as we were undressing to go to bed later and it stumbled about the wire tray chirruping angrily and sending unhatched eggs rolling all over the place.

"What a din," I grumbled to Maurice as I turned out the light but he was already asleep.

There were eleven chicks in the incubator in the morning, amid the debris. The only unhatched egg was misshaped.

"I shouldn't really have set that one," I said, "but we were short of eggs and I wanted a dozen."

"Never mind," he replied. "You've done jolly well."

I tidied up the incubator and took the six driest chicks out to the storeroom where Maurice had rigged up a brooder out of breeze blocks covered with a wire frame. Above it hung the infra-red lamp. The floor was covered with thick cardboard and sawdust. I set the chicks down carefully and looked at the thermometer. Stable at 95°, thank goodness.

The last egg hatched the same evening. The chick looked fine and slightly bigger than the others.

"100% fertilisation," said Maurice, impressed. "Good old Gandalf!"

"And 100% hatching in spite of everything. They must be more tolerant than we were led to think. But," I added, "never again in the bedroom. I wouldn't have believed such little creatures could make such a racket!"

The chicks thrived. I showed them how to eat and drink by gently pushing their beaks in the right direction and they cottoned on in a trice. I read that fresh chopped chives were good for growing chicks and they fell on them with gusto. By the time they were two weeks old they had become flighty and quarrelsome although I could not yet tell what sex they were.

"I do hope at least half of them are pullets," I said. "Perhaps I'd better start some more off, just in case."

"I've sold all our eggs to a camping boat," said Maurice.

"It doesn't matter – I'm not using ours, anyway. I'm going to try Marans this time." A neighbour had some pure bred birds including a handsome cockerel. "I was going to swap eggs with Yvonne but she won't mind waiting a day or so for ours. I'll pop along and fetch them now. By the time the next lot hatch these will be out in the garden."

The second hatching was less successful than the first which must have been beginner's luck. The incubator behaved quite well but we only ended up with seven healthy chicks. There were three unfertilised eggs, one dead chick (probably as a result of being booted about by previously hatched chicks) and one poor mite suffering from the dreaded 'sticky navel'.

The surviving Maran chicks were only a day old when near disaster struck!

Stephanie was home from Athens for a holiday at the time, and Bruce and Becky were staying for the weekend. We were all sitting in the parlour late on in the evening, exchanging anecdotes and looking at photographs. Suddenly we were plunged in darkness.

"A power cut!" exclaimed Maurice in exasperation. "I'll find some blankets to cover the freezers." He was remembering the first power failure we had had at Buckby Wharf. It continued for four days and our stock had not been insured.

"Never mind your ice-cream," I said, "what about my chicks!" I felt my way through the house to the stock-room where I found the torch hanging in its usual place and rushed outside. There was a stack of cardboard boxes near the back door, so I sorted out a smallish one and put an old towel in the bottom. Becky held the torch while I transferred the chicks, one by one, to the box. I closed the lid and carried the box indoors. It was a mild night but too cold for day-olds.

"Now what?" I looked at the anxious faces of the others in the candle-light. "How on earth can I keep them warm?"

"A hottie," suggested Stephanie, "under the blanket."

"How about putting the box in the airing cupboard?" said Becky.

"They'll probably be alright there for a bit," I said, closing the door of the airing cupboard, "but not if this wretched power cut goes on for long."

After what seemed like an age, we all trooped upstairs to inspect the chicks. They were huddled lethargically in a corner of the box.

"I'm sure they're getting cold," I said worriedly. If only we could get the bathroom really warm, somehow. "There's a calor gas heater in the shop," I said to Bruce, "d'you think you could bring it up here?"

"Sure. Bring the torch, Bex." Off they went.

With the stove installed in the bathroom and throwing out a tremendous heat, the room was soon like a furnace. We all sat sweating in a row on the edge of the bath listening to the chicks waking up and begin chirruping.

"They sound livelier," said Bruce. I nodded with relief which faded abruptly as the stove cut out with a loud click. There must have been a safety device which caused it to do this when it overheated.

"We'll let the room cool down a bit," I said, "and then relight the stove. But I don't fancy spending the whole night doing this!"

Luckily, we did not have to. The lights came on again around midnight and I took the chicks back to their brooder under the infra-red lamp. They looked perfectly happy the next day; showing no sign of their adventure.

our place looked like a poultry farm

The ice-cream was alright, too. But Maurice decided that it was time to get a generator. He had had enough of stressful power cuts, he said. Oddly enough, after he bought the generator which was capable of running a deepfreeze and several lights, it was three or four years before the power failed again.

By September, which was when I began this chicken saga, our place looked like a poultry farm. We had three separate hen coops on the lawn, one in the orchard, and two sets of hens free-ranging. Looking after them all took ages. The diets of different generations varied and those in the coops had to be given fresh greenstuff to make up for lack of grazing. We moved the runs daily to keep the ground sweet and the growing birds healthy.

As I expected, we ended up with more cocks than hens. Marans are big and heavy and make good table birds but the hybrid cockerels were tall and leggy. We were trying to fatten up seven of the latter in one run where they quarrelled incessantly. The Maran cockerels seemed to have more placid natures.

The pullets were allowed to free range and spent most of their time scuffling about in the herb garden, consuming vast quantities of chives and creepy-crawlies from the rockery surrounding it. The hybrids were better food gatherers than the Marans but they had the mistaken conviction that I was their mother. The moment I appeared out of the back door, they rushed up to me and clustered round – even perching on my shoulders and sitting on my feet so that I could scarcely take a step without tripping over. This belief persisted all their lives but as they matured the mother complex embraced all humans. It made walking about the orchard difficult for us all.

When the weather broke, it did so with a vengeance. Torrential rain beat down fiercely; stripping the petals off the roses and flattening the long grass in the wild garden. Ill equipped boaters dived into the shop to shelter from the rain while the lock filled; occasionally being persuaded to buy a waterproof. The Maran pullets rushed for cover the minute they felt the first fat drop of rain but the hybrids foraged on, regardless of their bedraggled plumage. They merely pointed their tail feathers downwards so that the water dripped off.

Towards the end of the month, some friends came to stay – people we had known many years before when Maurice was a serving officer in the army. George and Christina lived in Edinburgh and we had not seen them for a long time. One of the unusual things about George is that he has the gift of water-divining. He is a dowser. When he first told us about this, we were both rather sceptical and unkindly set him a test which he passed with flying colours. We lived in Hampshire then, in a large house built of flint and chalk. In the middle of the kitchen floor was a well which was reputed to be over eighty feet deep. We had dropped a pebble in it once and never heard it reach the bottom.

George did not know about the well. When we bought the house, the kitchen floor was covered with lino which we replaced with something newer. I did not want two adventurous children even suspecting that there was a well underneath!

The house was surrounded by hazel trees which gave it its name of Hazelhurst. George found himself a suitable hazel twig, (Y shaped, I think) and wandered around the place holding the twig in front of him. After about ten minutes he approached the back door saying that there was no water to speak of in the garden. Suddenly the twig started dipping and twitching and he came into the kitchen. I could see his knuckles whitening as he sought to control the antics of the twig.

"You'll never credit this," he said in his lilting Scottish voice, "but there's a lot of water underneath your kitchen floor."

As we walked around the garden at Buckby Wharf with George and Christina, I told them of my wish to create a bog and pond for wildlife.

"Not a smart pool with goldfish," I explained, "but one for newts and frogs and dragonflies and things. I would have liked to dam a natural stream but our soil is too free-draining. It'll have to be an artificial pond."

"D'you want me to see if I can find you a stream?" asked George.

"Yes please!" I said, thrilled at the idea. "But I don't really want to break a twig off my little hazel bushes."

"No matter," said George, "a wire coat-hanger will do."

"We've plenty of those," I said and fetched one without delay.

He found three streams running diagonally across the lawn from south-west to north-east. Unfortunately, they were not anywhere near the place I had in mind for the pond, which was in the wild garden. One stream went straight through the soft fruit cage and another through the island bed of old-fashioned roses (Maurice had rudely referred to the latter as 'what you choose to call a rose-garden' when I planted it and the name had stuck!). The third and weakest response George got seemed to be heading straight for the driveway. There was another snag.

"I can tell you there's water flowing," said George, "but not how deep underground it is. It could be a long way down."

"Hm," I murmured thoughtfully. "I hadn't bargained for a bore-hole. Perhaps we'd better shelve the idea for the time being. Thanks anyway."

Maurice had dispatched one of the hybrid cockerels to provide curried chicken for George and Christina. I grimaced when he produced the headless corpse with a polythene bag enclosing its bloodied neck.

"What on earth have you done to it?" I asked.

"I've cut its head off," he said. "I thought it was better to do that than try and wring its neck and not do it properly."

I did not say much, just switched on the omnibus edition of the Archers to take my mind off what I was doing. I had only plucked one chicken before and that was Aragorn, our first rooster. Bruce had helped me then and I recalled using pliers to pull out the flight feathers. This one took me about two hours to pluck and draw – with the stock-holder's book propped in front of me. I collected the feathers in a paper sack and then tipped them into the compost bin. Lucifer, our cat, insinuated himself into the stock-room and watched eagerly as I sorted out the giblets from the rest of the innards. When it was all over, a chicken dish was the last thing either of us wanted to see on the menu!

I got quicker with practice, of course. By the time I got to the seventeenth, I had cut the time down to twenty minutes. But it temporarily spoilt my appetite for poultry. I needed to put the birds in the freezer for three months before I could cook and eat my share with any semblance of enjoyment.

As for Maurice – his part in the messy business was far more unpleasant and he hated it. Luckily Yvonne came by as I was plucking the second headless bird.

"Good heavens!" she said. "I'll show him how to do it properly." She went off into the orchard and within a couple of minutes I had two more birds to pluck, both with dangling heads intact. She also showed me how to truss them neatly, which was something I had not bothered too much about. They were only for home consumption, generally coq au vin or curry, hardly ever roast. Cocks are dark and flavoursome with less white meat than hens – but tougher. I gave the last and biggest bird (unplucked!) to the lock-keeper as a thank-you for his offer of feeding the livestock when we were away.

This was to be the first year since we began trading as Ginger's Canal Stores that we would shut the shop for the winter. We had been arguing about this ever since Blisworth tunnel reopened and our takings had rocketed. Not that the place would ever make us millionaires, you understand, but at last we were beginning to feel that our previous efforts might pay off after all. Maurice was less keen on the idea than me. He felt that we had a duty to our customers to stay open all the year round. Unfortunately, boaters were few in the winter and bought little – mainly perishables which were the very items we did not want to stock when business was slack. If, as we hoped at first, we had become the indispensable village shop to local people it might have persuaded us. But Buckby Wharf was a hamlet, not a village, and its population too scattered to make ours a convenience store. The locals had scarcely used us.

"Our turnover this winter will be chicken feed compared with the summer," I predicted.

"What about your painted ware? It's always been popular as Christmas presents," he said.

"Hm." I glanced round the shop and up at the empty hooks on the ceiling. "We started the season with masses and I've never stopped painting all year. Look! It's practically all gone. I'd find it much easier to build up a good supply for next season if we cleared out the shop and turned it into a work-room for the winter. We could hang a thick curtain over the door and make it really cosy, too. At the moment, whenever a lorry driver comes in for a Mars bar, fifty pence worth of heat flies out with him!"

"O.K.," he sighed resignedly, "you win. I must admit I'm weary after a seven day week for nine months on the trot. We'll shut straight after the autumn half term."

"I'll put a sign to that effect in the window to warn everybody," I said, pleased. "We could even have a holiday!"

= 4 =

THAMES TRAVELS

Maurice put down the phone with a grimace. Drought conditions were still affecting many waterways and he had just rung the British Waterways area office to check on the situation. It was obviously not to his liking.

"If you add scheduled stoppages for maintenance to the ones due to water shortage, there's little point in our going away on the boat this winter," he said morosely.

"Ironic, isn't it?" I commented bitterly. "Our first real taste of freedom in five years and the canals have to dry up!"

"Things may improve by the spring," he said, unfolding the route planner. This is an essential piece of kit. It is a map of the whole waterway system marked off in sections, each of which is given a set of three numbers stating mileage, number of locks and average cruising time for the section. You decide how many hours cruising you expect to put in each day for how ever many days and plan your route to fit. This time, Maurice was using the planner initially to work out if we could go anywhere at all! He pencilled in the stoppages and the dates of their duration on the map.

"We ought to reopen the shop a full week before Good Friday next year, don't you think?" I asked.

"Definitely," he agreed, poring over the map. "Most of the planned restrictions should be lifted in time to give us ten days at the end of March if we get everything ready here before we leave. It's cutting it fine but better than no cruise at all. It also depends on the reservoirs filling up by then but we can only hope for the best."

"Well, I suppose we'd better get on with producing the goods for next season," I said glumly. "Then at least we can go away with a clear conscience."

However, it was pleasant to have some time to ourselves and we both cheered up as soon as we got into our new routine. The shop premises made an excellent studio. With the shelves cleared of groceries – an easy task as most of it had been sold in the flurry of trade during half-term – and the electric till stowed underneath the counter, we had ample work space. The stacks of blue and white boxes containing enamel ware waiting to be decorated were a daunting sight but I was anxious to make a start on them. Maurice's function in the production line was priming and backgrounding galvanised goods and this could not happen until we had collected our order from the tinsmith in Birmingham. So we wasted no time in doing that; loading the cans, dippers and scoops into the Suzuki and rattling our way home on the M.6.

"It's a good job, in a way," said Maurice," that the order wasn't complete. We'd never have fitted any more in the jeep."

"It means another trip, though" I said, "to fetch the three-gallon cans. I reckon we need a trailer."

"I was thinking the same last August when we were so busy. I could bring back a week's supply of groceries from the Cash and Carry in one go. It would save petrol, too."

"There's a place in Northampton which makes trailers," I said. "If we bought one large enough for sheep, we wouldn't be dependent on other people fetching them at dipping and tupping time."

We had four ewes, all Jacobs. Rachel and Leah were our original two and we had kept one ewe lamb from each of them. Mistake was Rachel's daughter and earned her name by constantly getting herself into scrapes. Some sheep may be stupid but Jacobs are goat-like and canny. Mistake's first escapade as a lamb had been to get herself stuck in the fork of an apple tree while trying to eat leaves beyond her reach! Her latest trick was to leap onto the roof of the large henhouse, do a little dance and then sail off the other side with an upward kick of her back feet. She had a thick, luxurious fleece, an aristocratic Roman nose and upward flaring horns.

"Mistake's by far the tallest of the four," I added, "so let's measure her."

"Easier said than done," said Maurice, after several attempts. "Let's try Sooty and add an inch or two."

Mistake's half-sister stood docilely while Maurice waved the steel tape around her and I jotted down the figures. But then, as a parting shot, she jabbed him with her sharp, downward pointing horns.

"Ouch!" he grunted. "Half-rations of pellets for you tonight, miss."

The mobile shepherd rolled up the next day to fetch the ewes for tupping. They were going to run with his flock of Suffolks. It struck me after they had gone that we had no idea where he was taking them.

"Wouldn't it be awful if we never saw them again?"

"I'm not so sure," said Maurice, rubbing his backside ruefully. "When d'you reckon they'll lamb? I'd forgotten about that when I was planning our spring cruise."

"Oh, not until late April," I said. "Yvonne will keep an eye on them until we get back."

It rained off and on throughout November and we began to feel hopeful about our holiday, even going out for the day once or twice on Warwickshire Lad to detect problems which might have arisen during the long months of disuse. We grasped the opportunity to collect any floating timber we saw and bring it back for the stove. A huge dead elm had come down on the Leicester Arm; falling right across the canal and the towpath. A Waterways team had cut out the middle section to allow free passage for boats but the towpath was still blocked. So we took Warwickshire Lad along, armed with a chainsaw, and did a public service by sawing up as much as possible and loading it on the roof.

"It seems a pity to leave the rest of the tree floating there," said Maurice. He rummaged in the well and emerged with a length of rope, its end spliced into a loop. I watched nervously as he balanced himself precariously on the half-submerged trunk and eventually lassoed a branch. With much effort and a lot of swearing and slithering, he managed to draw the tree in to the side. Just as I thought he had done it, the whole thing rolled over and the branch embedded itself and our rope firmly in the mud. Pull as we might, we could not shift it.

Maurice cursed loudly. "That's a good rope!"

"Hm! You'll have to cut off the loop, which is a pity." Neither of us were much good at splicing, unfortunately.

"Not if I can help it!" He stripped down to his underpants – what a sight in chilly November! – and waded in, plunging his arms into the ooze to try and free the rope. But it was no good. "Pass me my Swiss Army knife," he said regretfully. Then he hauled himself onto the bank, filthy and shivering. "Nicholas spliced that loop," he said as he coiled up the rest of the rope and chucked it inboard, "when we were on the Thames, remember?"

what a sight

"Perfectly," I replied dryly, casting my mind back to a summer cruise many years before when we had been accompanied by a French lad on an exchange visit with Stephanie.

Nicholas had not wanted to come and stay with us at all, we discovered soon after he arrived. He had no desire whatsoever to learn how to speak our language and absolutely no interest in sightseeing in England. He informed us of the latter as we set out for Warwick Castle! Nicholas, in fact, was bored stiff when he was not ocean sailing and he laid the blame for his wasted vacation on his father.

"Whatever can we do with him?" I whispered to Maurice after three days of black scowls and sulky silence.

"Bring our holiday forward and take him on the inland waterways," grunted Maurice. "If he's so mad about sailing he should enjoy it."

"Warwickshire Lad isn't a yacht," I said dubiously.

"They're all boats. He'll be fine on board, you'll see"

We were determined to instil some knowledge of our country into the wretched boy whether he liked it or not, so we decided to aim for the river Thames and London, thinking it would be more to his liking than the quieter northern canals. It would be a first time for us as well.

He was very supercilious at the start; scorning our lack of sail and praising the skill of yachtsmen over mere boaters. Even the locks fell far short, in his estimation, of those in France and he was probably right there. The French canals were built for larger vessels and are better maintained. Many of them are still used for commercial traffic. But some of the cockiness went out of Nicholas when he stood at the top of Hatton 21 looking down the flight.

"*Où se trouve Madame l'éclusière?*" he asked, his dark eyebrows raised. Stephanie grinned and shook her head which he took to mean that he was supposed to speak in English. He made a stab at it. "Where ees the Mrs of the locks finding herself?"

"No such luck." Bruce gave him a windlass and crossed to the other side of the chamber. Nicholas looked helplessly at the paddle gear until Stephanie took pity on him. Maurice told him the Thames would be different, but thank goodness we had tamed him by the time we reached the river. He put himself in charge of ropes; coiling flat any he saw lying around, shocked at the cavalier way in which we slung them on board when we let go from a mooring. This criticism was accepted as justified. Then he asked permission, instantly given, to splice a new cotton line. He made a turk's head (which someone stole recently) to fit on the swan's neck of the tiller and checked every scrap of rope we possessed for signs of frayed ends which he corrected.

"Thank heavens," I murmured to Stephanie as we left the Oxford Canal and swung sharp right into Duke's Cut, "Nicholas is O.K. at last."

"Mind your heads!" yelled Maurice to the two boys standing in the front of the boat, tongues wagging in a blend of French and English. The lads ducked just in time but the front of the cratch caught the left side of the narrow brick bridge carrying the towpath. There was a sound of cracking timber. "I approached at the wrong angle," admitted Maurice. "It's a tighter turn than it looks. What's the damage?"

"You've broken the cabin block," called Bruce in dismay as we emerged from under the arch. The impact had pushed the triangular cratch, to which the front of the walking plank was secured, backwards. The other end of the plank was firmly seated on the cabin roof by means of a sturdy block nine inches high and two inches thick. It was this which had borne the brunt of the blow and split doing so. Without it, the whole edifice above the well would collapse. And while Nicholas was our guest, Bruce's bed was underneath. No wonder he looked worried.

"I'll mend it when we stop for lunch," said Maurice irritably, "no need to stare at me so accusingly, Bruce."

The repair was quickly and efficiently done by using two long screws and a pair of angled brackets. It won't be the block that cracks next time, I thought. It will be the cabin!

We ascended the only lock on the Duke of Marlborough's Canal (Duke's Cut) which raised us a foot or so, it varies according to the level of the river. Four hundred yards later we emerged from the invading undergrowth into the weir stream of King's Lock and turned upriver.

Having gone to the trouble and expense of getting a Thames licence, we thought we would get the full value out of it by cruising north to Lechlade before turning south again towards London.

And what a palaver it was to get that registration certificate, I remember. Because we had made a last minute decision to cruise the Thames, there was insufficient time to untie all the red tape before we left home. So we asked a friend to collect the licence for us from Nugent House in Reading and send it to Kidlington Post Office where we collected it *en route*. There were several anxious moments spent waiting for the clerk to find the envelope addressed to us among all the others.

As for cost – I thought that one half of the annual charge for a fifteen day visitor's licence was unfair and designed to keep visitors away. I expect it did.

We had also gone to quite a lot of trouble to comply with Thames Conservancy bylaws which constituted a list as long as your arm; covering the construction and equipment of 'motor launches' in great detail. The gas cooker had to be chained to the bulkhead, for instance, and the sink outlet sealed although quite what they expected you to do with your washing-up water I never discovered. I used to give deserving bushes a soaking with ours but I never saw anyone else doing the same. I guess they just slung it over the side!

No one ever checked up on us so perhaps we need not have bothered. One of the most awkward rules for which failure to comply was a criminal offence was that the boat's name had to be displayed on either side of the bow and on the stern. Chris Barney had built most of his craft, including ours, with attractive oval name boards screwed to both cabin sides. The best I could do in the time was to write Warwickshire Lad very large in felt pen on three pieces of cardboard and stick them with blue-tack in the appropriate places! They got soggy and disintegrated after the first squall but we kept patching them up and sticking them back in order to stay out of prison. I was thankful to get rid of them in a rubbish bin at Brentford.

The upper reaches of the Thames are peaceful and pastoral. There is insufficient headroom under Osney Bridge in Oxford for ocean-going cruisers, so other boats are few and far between. The river is narrow and friendly; meandering between watermeadows filled with dairy herds. The bends are sometimes so extravagant that although we could see a moored boat about five miles away as the crow flies, it was a good four hours before we passed it.

We knew Lechlade well from the road; passing through it regularly on our way to visit parents in Poole. The traffic lights on Halfpenny Bridge were invariably red: many is the time I have sat there; waiting for them to change, enviously looking at the boats on the river. From there it is just possible to see St John's Lock where Father Thames reclines in front of the cottage.

On this occasion, we had tied the boat up at the free moorings alongside the meadow before shopping in the town. Bruce was somewhat put out when his headmaster strolled by with his wife and dog. He did not exactly stand to attention but he took his hands out of his pockets! We pushed on (Bruce at the tiller) for the final half mile to the navigational limit for powered craft where Bruce swung us expertly round in midstream before giving a farewell salute to his mentor. Then, it was a good lunch at The Trout in their sunny garden before heading back to Oxford.

Attractive pubs are numerous on the Thames and their moorings welcoming. We only had one disappointment which shall be nameless. Its jetty submerged beneath Maurice's weight (in the dark!) and he actually found the beer so horrible that he could not drink it. I cannot recall that ever happening before or since.

We spent two nights on the Upper Thames and it was about eighteen cruising hours before we arrived once more at the entrance to Duke's Cut on our way south. There was no doubt that we travelled faster going downstream, using less fuel, but the rule that locks be left empty at all times slowed us down a lot as we always had to fill them. Osney Bridge did not threaten our newly repaired cabin block and Nicholas displayed no particular satisfaction at finding that the locks were now mechanised and operated by a uniformed lock-keeper.

We tied up below Folly Bridge, after swinging round to face upstream. The sweet Thames was running so softly, however, that the precaution was probably unnecessary. Into Oxford we went, not to shop but to show Nicholas around our oldest university town. He was obviously impressed – even buying himself an Oxford University tee-shirt and dozens of postcards destined for France. In fact, he was enjoying himself so much that we spent the whole day sight-seeing, finishing up with the Ashmolean museum and remaining at our mooring for the night.

This turned out to be a mistake. Dawn's rosy fingers had scarcely caressed the eastern sky when we were all rudely awoken by a horrendous din. A voice, no further away than eighteen inches at the most, was bellowing through a megaphone. With barely a pause for breath, it hollered. The words were indistinguishable but the tone was officious and undoubtedly offensive. I could not understand why no-one answered back until suddenly the shouting stopped and I heard the crunch of cycle tyres and splashing of oars.

"Eights," I moaned, taking my fingers out of my ears. "I suppose that dreadful row was made by the coach. I bet he parked himself by our boat on purpose." I rolled off the bed and put on the kettle. "What about an early start as we're all wide awake?"

We had the last laugh when we got to Maidenhead the following weekend and found ourselves in the middle of a regatta. Warwickshire Lad was permitted to cruise slowly between a line of markers and the bank but the competitors objected to the slight wash we created and the coxes shot us evil looks. As for the gin and tonic brigade on the velvet lawns, they did not approve of us at all. Maurice was not wearing a peaked cap with gold braid and above the well a line of washing flapped merrily. Added to that, we had a better view of the race than they did.

Nothing much happened between Oxford and Reading except that one hot afternoon Bruce fell asleep at the tiller. I remember it vividly because I was sunbathing on the roof at the time. It was a nasty shock suddenly to find myself buried in the depths of a weeping willow with the bow of the boat stuck firmly in the bank. Bruce woke with a start but no-one else did. Between us we extricated ourselves without the rest of the crew being any the wiser.

It was about 10 a.m. on another warm morning when we turned into Kennet Mouth and tied up at Crane Wharf. We filled up with water at the Reading Marine Co. who kindly said that we were welcome to leave the boat there while we shopped in the town. We had originally intended to slip back out afterwards and proceed on our way down the Thames but something drew us on – as so frequently happens. We found ourselves going through Blake's Lock, the only Thames Conservancy lock which is not actually on the Thames. Above it, there seemed to be some sort of drama being enacted by police frogmen. No one was keen to tell us what was going on but we heard murmurings about a toddler lost overboard.

We had one or two anxious moments during the nine miles of River Kennet. The fast-flowing water (in spite of low rainfall) through the narrow, twisty Brewery Cut was hair-raising and unexpected. We were mightily glad we did not meet anything coming the other way. A brief stop at the Cunning Man (Maurice noted in the log the excellence of their Courage beer!) calmed us down for the next crisis.

We had been warned that the turf-sided locks made getting on and off the boat difficult but having never seen this type of lock it was not easy to understand the implications. So we zoomed in, looped the ropes fore and aft on the handy metal piles and got about the business of opening paddles and taking photographs. Then – lo – the lock was full. The turf, piles, ropes and all had disappeared beneath the water; leaving the boat a yard out from the side!

It was a hot day. My ankles were puffy and feet swollen. So off with shoes and socks and in I waded to retrieve the situation. In fact, the cool water lapping the short grass felt so delicious that I paddled in all the turf-sided locks after that, and very sad I felt to read that their days were numbered.

Sulhampstead Swing Bridge caused us a lot of trouble. Maurice described it in the log as a 'pig' and it was no better on the way back. If it had not been so difficult to shift, we would not have made the mistake we did when we got to Tile Mill Swing Bridge. After Maurice, Bruce and Nicholas had struggled with it for about ten minutes, they gave up and we turned back.

"It must be locked," grumbled Bruce. It was ages before we discovered that it was actually the limit of navigation at that time. Fortunately, there was no-one about to witness our ignorance. We returned to the Cunning Man and tied up for the night. I have to confess that Maurice was not the only one to sample the Courage – I think we all did, even Nicholas.

The foray up the Kennet over, we continued our journey downstream towards Henley; stopping around lunchtime at Val Wyatt's boatyard, situated where the unnavigable Hennerton Backwater loops off into Templecombe Wood. Stephanie and I explored the shop while the others dealt with refuelling, gas and so on. None of us noticed immediately that one of our dogs was missing when Warwickshire Lad eventually nosed out into midstream.

"Tansy must have jumped off at the boatyard," I said.

When we got back there was no sign of the welsh terrier. Then suddenly I saw something thrashing about in the water actually *inside* a large boathouse on the opposite side of the basin. Thankfully, a woman walking past caught sight of the animal and managed to get hold of her collar. She hoisted Tansy onto the concrete but the dog just stood there, exhausted. I ran round the basin, calling, until Tansy's addled brain responded and she slithered under the wire towards me.

"She's O.K." I said to the others. "Thank goodness she had a new collar." I always checked the dog collars before a cruise - it has saved their lives on several occasions.

It was much later than usual when we tied up that evening. We worked ourselves through Boveney Lock after the keeper had gone off duty. This meant that the power was turned off. An electrically powered Thames lock without any electricity is more hard graft than the whole of Buckby flight, in my view. It was pitch dark when we finally emerged.

"Here!" called Bruce from the front of the boat where he had been scanning the bank for a likely mooring. He jumped off with the rope and

I tossed him a mooring spike which was quickly hammered in. Nicholas followed with the stern rope and shortly we were snugly settled. Supper was cooked, eaten and cleared away. Not long after that all of us were tucked up in bed and soundly asleep.

It must have been two in the morning when I dreamt I could hear music. Jazz. One of my favourite tunes. I turned over, smiled, went back to sleep. Dimly, in my dreams, voices called and water slapped against the hull. The boat rocked.

When the saints, go marching in. When the saints go marching in. I want to be, among their number, when the saints go marching in.

"What the....?" asked Maurice as the saints escalated in volume. Noses pressed against the glass, we stared out of misty windows at the passing trip boat; gyrating figures bopping drunkenly to the frenzied beat, oblivious of being watched by sleepy, sober eyes. And then, as suddenly as it had appeared, the vision vanished into the lock chamber and the gates cut off the sound. Vaguely, I thought of the crew interminably winding, winding, winding.....until I slept.

Three-thirty a.m.

When the saints, go marching in. When the saints go marching in. I want to be, among their number, when the saints go marching in.

I pulled the bedclothes up over my head. No one else in our boat stirred as we rolled in the wash and sounds of New Orleans faded into the distance.

Fresh morning light hazed with the promise of a hot day sparkled on an expanse of green sward.

"Jolly nice place," observed Bruce as he poked his nose out of the stern doorway first thing. "Posh houses over on the other bank. Miles of empty grass with a smart white fence in the distance. There's even a little wood too. I'm going outside."

"Put the kettle on first," I wheedled.

"I'm sorry to say," he announced apologetically five minutes later, "because I chose this mooring – but I think we ought to push off fairly fast."

"I haven't had my cup of tea yet," I complained.

"Not now, Mother," he said. When Bruce says 'Mother' he means business. "There are signboards everywhere prohibiting mooring and an extremely angry-looking man heading this way. I'll yank out the spikes before he gets here – I hope."

"Make sure both dogs are on board first," I yawned as Maurice started the engine. "What a night!" Remembering, I hummed softly to myself as I pulled on my clothes.

Even now, a decade and a half later, I never hear 'The Saints' being played on the radio without recalling that night at Windsor Racecourse.

= 5 =

BRUM TRIP

The shepherd brought our ewes back on the fifth of January. There had been a hard frost the night before and a sprinkling of snow so there was not much grass for them to eat.

"We're in for a lot more of this," announced the shepherd knowledgeably, glancing at the dark ochre sky.

"I'll get in some extra hay then," said Maurice.

Frost is more of an aggravation to a small-holder than snow. Snow blankets the ground; keeping autumn sown broad beans and winter cauliflower plants snug. Hens can eat snow but ice is no good to sheep or fowl. Every morning and evening we went out with a bucket of tepid water from the tap to fill the tub and the drinkers. The wheels of the big henhouse froze to the ground and Maurice needed a crowbar to shift it. Treacherous ice everywhere made it hard to keep one's feet about the place. The canal froze.

More snow fell. Then there was a bright, clear morning when I crunched along the towpath to paint a watercolour of the wooden footbridge at the junction. I saw cat's footprints on the ice and hoped they were not Lucifer's. The air was pricklingly cold in my nostrils, the canal sparkled and bushes were rimed with frost. Further along the Leicester Arm, the snow had drifted in high ridges making it impossible to tell where towpath ended and canal began. Surely this will fill the reservoirs, I thought.

Rain cleared the snow at the end of January but more thick, wet flakes fell the following month. I had to shake young conifers free of the weight which threatened to snap them. This time the snow settled only briefly before it melted and soaked into the earth.

Now I was confidently looking forward to our holiday. Unscheduled restrictions were being lifted. We could cope with the rest.

Our cottage seemed oddly empty when we set off for the eagerly awaited cruise on Warwickshire Lad. For the first time we were not dependent on our long-suffering family to give us a break.

"I'll see the hens are alright," said the lock-keeper, "and Lucifer. Have a good trip."

It was drizzly and cold along the exposed stretch between Braunston Turn and Napton Junction. To our dismay, British Waterways had cut down all the wonderful crab-apple trees which had been growing along the towpath between the junction and Calcutt top lock. We had had so much fruit from those trees in the past that I was fond of them even though we now owned a John Downie and a Golden Hornet. Annoyed, we went on a bit further to tie up just after Gibraltar Bridge. The private moorings opposite intrigued me. The boats look shabby and neglected and the place has always been deserted. And yet the land around a reedy offshoot of the canal has been fashioned into a quaint and exciting garden. There are narrow mown paths winding in an out of trees and bushes, interplanted with bulbs and woodland flowers: a magic garden in which a child could play make-believe.

Rain poured on us as we worked down Stockton locks. Steering, I had to peer through the curtain of water running off my sou'wester to see at all. When we got to Welsh Road lock the heavens really opened and I was momentarily blinded. I could not even tell what I had hit until the rain eased off. It turned out to be a big black boat called Raven, tied up alongside the lawn of the lock cottage. Fortunately, no one was on board at the time and no accusing eyes stared at me from the cottage window. I put a gumbooted foot on the wooden hull and silently shoved us off. Neither boat seemed to have suffered from the impact. Maurice was ineffectually sheltering under an oak tree.

He grinned. "Having fun on the dodgems?"

In the afternoon the sky began to lighten, thank goodness. We like to think we are not fair-weather boaters but there comes a time when you are past caring how wet you are; when you stop noticing the dribbles running down your neck and soaking your jumper; when it trickles off your waterproof trousers into your boots and you cannot be bothered to change your soggy socks; when you squelch through the boat from front to back heedless of the pools you are making on the floor.

The rain cleared as we mounted the first four locks of Hatton 21 to tie up in the long pound at dusk. Another boat was there before us; ghostly in the mist rising from the water.

"It'll be fine tomorrow," said Maurice, "you'll see." He pulled the canopy down over the well and hung our wet things on the line to dry in the warmth of the Tilley lamp which he lit. Inside the cabin, the Squirrel stove popped and crackled cheerfully. Soon we were dry and warm.

Sure enough, the twenty-one golden steps to heaven of Hatton were bathed in sunlight the next morning. It shone on our freshly painted Buckby can and the flowers in the Aylesbury can. I had found time before we left to pick a bunch of early daffodils. They seemed to have enjoyed being drenched!

The level at the top of Hatton was down, as it so often was. The twenty-one wide locks were greedy enough, but I think a lot of water disappeared from the Grand Union at Kingswood Junction to fall down through the leaky locks of the Southern Stratford. We have noticed an improvement since the National Trust handed over responsibility of the latter to British Waterways.

In spite of 'the bottom being too near the top', Maurice managed to creep past the moorings belonging to the South Warwickshire Yacht Club with scarcely a ripple. They are very pernickety about such things. Meanwhile, I went below to prepare a meal. There was ample time as the moorings continue for half a mile.

We paused for a while at White bridge for me to sketch. I had done the same view once before, when the trees glittered in their brilliant autumn colours: a rich tapestry of green and gold through which the sun filtered onto the purple brickwork, conjuring up crimson streaks. This time the light was pale and cold, the branches leafless.

The great tree opposite Kingswood Junction stood with its roots only partially exposed. The first time we had negotiated the sharp turn under the railway bridge we had gone firmly aground on the sand bar created by the tangle of roots. Now a brand new finger post is firmly embedded in the mud, placed there by Doug Smith, the bicycling cartographer of canal maps.

Maurice and I discussed which way we should go from here. We had already decided to go to Birmingham ultimately.

"The north Stratford's prettier," I said. "Although I can't say I'm keen on doing the Hatton *and* the Lapworth flight in the same day. On the other hand, I don't much want to stop here overnight because the railway's so noisy."

"If we continue on the Grand Union," said Maurice, "there's only the five locks at Knowle to do today. We can stop at that pleasant mooring where we often used to tie up when we lived in Moseley."

"The painting spot? I remember." Our permanent mooring in those days had been at Copt Heath Wharf. Whenever we spent the weekend working on the boat, we had moved it to the same quiet, rural place where unbroken coping stones edged the canal and the towpath was broad and level. Bruce amused himself in a canoe and the dogs snuffled around enjoying themselves. There was a holiday atmosphere even though we were beavering away with sandpaper and yacht enamel. I recall one night there when we were kept awake by a shoal of minnows noisily eating algae off the hull.

"Knowle it shall be then," I agreed. "But you'll have to work the locks while I steer. I don't suppose the paddle gear's got any easier since we were last up this way. The top lock always defeated me."

Our first stop the following day was at Catty Barnes for a warm loaf from the bakery and a pint of milk. Then it was goodbye to the countryside and hullo to Brum, our old stamping ground.

I get very irritated when I hear about boaters going to tremendous lengths to avoid the city on their travels or whizzing through as quickly as possible on the New Main Line without a glance to right or left. The Birmingham Canal Navigations, or B.C.N. for short, is central to the English canal system; embracing much of the industrial Midlands. It should be relished not avoided. Although not all the original one hundred and sixty miles of waterway is open to boats today, its extent is only surpassed by Bangkok. In my opinion every boater worth his salt cruises the B.C.N. occasionally. It is not such a tall order either. We negotiated every navigable route, loop and arm of it one Easter. It was early on in our boating career and we have since retraced parts of it many times. It is always an adventure. Sadly, we have seen a number of old wharves and warehouses 'developed' or demolished over the years. So hasten there now – while there is still some of our industrial history left!

We were having a lazy day so tied up short of Camp Hill locks at Golden Hillock bridge, another favourite mooring from the old days. It is alongside a sports ground and used to be screened from the railway sidings by a gun factory. You get to know, if you cruise the B.C.N. regularly, which factories work all night and which do not; and of the former, which ones shut down at weekends and bank holidays. Tyseley

Wharf, for instance, is tolerable on Saturday nights but to be avoided on any others because the shunting yards make the devil of a din!

"Remember what happened the last time we tied up here?" asked Maurice as he hammered in the mooring spikes.

We had set off for a summer cruise on the Friday evening. Bruce and I left home in the Beetle for Copt Heath Wharf in the early afternoon to get Warwickshire Lad ready, and Maurice joined us as soon as he could. We started along the fifteen mile pound towards Camp Hill with no fixed idea how far we would get before dark. The days were long and there were no restrictions on the locks.

We had left Solihull behind when Maurice uneasily announced that he could not remember locking the front door.

"We're actually nearer home now than we were when we started," I said. "Let's tie up at Golden Hillock bridge. I'll get supper while you nip home on the bike and check that everything's O.K."

"Yes," he said, looking relieved. "I'll do that."

"He's longer than I expected," I said to Bruce when supper was on the table.

"Yeah. I'm starving."

We waited another half hour and then Bruce ate his meal. The sun slid down the sky.

"It'll be dark soon," I said worriedly, "and the bike doesn't have lights." It was dusk before we heard the rattle of the old folding bicycle coming down the towpath. "At last!" My voice cracked with relief. "Why were you so long?"

"We've been burgled!" Maurice replied grimly. "They must've been frightened off before I got there. I followed the trail through the house as far as our bedroom."

"What's been taken," I asked, dreading his reply.

"T.V.," he said. "Tape-recorders, radios."

"My stereo?" Bruce's forehead crinkled with anxiety. He had spent his vacation reading gas-meters to buy it.

"No. They didn't get as far as the second floor. It's a pity they took the reel-to-reel, though. They're obsolete and we've all those reels we'll never be able to play again." This sad prophecy has been fulfilled. Maurice thought he had found a replacement machine recently in a junk shop, but it turned out to be two track instead of four. It sounded gibberish!

"Anything else stolen?"

"Yes," said Maurice regretfully. "My sword and medals. Now I must go back. There's no window so I'll have to sleep on the sofa." He yawned and went outside. "I remembered to put some lights on the bike. See you tomorrow – whenever..." He swung his leg over the saddle and looked back. "And by the way – I *had* locked the front door."

Maurice and I reminisced about the burglary during the evening at Golden Hillock's bridge before we slept. It did not seem nearly as peaceful a mooring as hitherto and we woke early. It's good to be back in narrow locks, I thought, as we dropped down Camp Hill. They are less effort for two. The boat does not swing from one side to the other and I bravely did what Maurice and Bruce always do – open one lower gate and then step across the gap to the other. It saves the effort of walking round the tail of the lock. I dare not look down though!

I have always been fond of Camp Hill flight; an oasis nestling in the middle of an industrial desert. Stuff has seeded there from all over the place – blown by the wind, dropped by birds, drifted on the water, thrown there by people getting rid of garden rubbish. There are the usual plants which take over disturbed ground; nettles, rosebay willow herb, Oxford ragwort and golden rod. Then there are wizened shrubs; lilac, buddleia and cotoneaster. Dandelions, purple loosestrife, watermint, honesty and many more nectar-rich flowers grow in profusion. And because of these, the butterflies have moved in – small tortoiseshell and peacock. I have seen blackberries, tomatoes and rhubarb growing there too, although not on the same occasion.

This time, it was dog violets which abounded. I picked a tiny bunch of them and a few coltsfoot for the cabin while I was waiting.

The only lock on the flight I dislike is the one under the railway line and thank goodness it has now been relocated. Trains thundering overhead give me the jitters and it looked such a frail old structure viewed from underneath, I often wondered whether it might give way! In wet weather, the bridge leaked gallons of water; not so much like a sieve as a funnel – directed on the unfortunate boater winding up the ground paddle!

The bottom lock opens onto Bordesley Junction; a sharp right-hander if one is making for Garrison flight and its obstacle course of rubbish. We were given a dose of that not long before so headed north. Here, old warehouses look down forbiddingly as they have done for decades, but the cheerful sight of a colourful narrow boat topped with flowers brought many a smiling face to the grimy windows high above us. I have often seen a full rubbish boat tied up in one of the old loading bays, presumably left there by Caggie Stevens and his canal horse.

Then we were swallowed up by the short tunnel under the railway lines to be regurgitated at the bottom lock of the next flight. Ashted locks have quite a different flavour from Camp Hill; instead of being sheltered and narrowly enclosed within mellow brick walls, there are grassy spaces around the broad, litter-strewn pounds between the locks. Through the vandal-proof wire guarding the towpath, you catch a glimpse along an alley of people and traffic. The wind whistles through, too, even in summer. It is a relief to leave the flight behind and turn left at Aston Junction onto the Birmingham and Fazeley Canal.

We passed under Old Snow Hill; musical instruments visible inside the windows of the building on top of the bridge. Then we were underneath Livery Street and entering the bowels of Birmingham.

The Farmer's Bridge flight of locks ascend steeply to the heart of the city. The pounds are wide to allow for overflow; water sneaking under buildings and lapping at the feet of the Post Office Tower rising above the insignificant boater. The non-towpath side of the lower locks are surrounded by water, so that each is a peninsula. The light was dim; filtering spasmodically between the tall buildings which overshadow the flight or straddle it entirely. The atmosphere was dank and mysterious. When the water level is high, headroom is low and navigating needs care. The cratch on Warwickshire Lad has been perilously close on one or two occasions. This time, only the flowers in the Aylesbury can brushed the underside of the concrete span above us although we had taken the precaution of lowering the chimney.

We emerged into weak sunshine for the last four locks; delighted to see someone opening the paddles of the one ahead, prior to coming down. Until that minute every single lock had been against us.

"We'll have done twenty-five locks when we get to the top of these," I said hopefully to Maurice.

"Want to knock off?"

"Yes. I'd like a mooch round town."

We tied up at Cambrian Wharf, pleased to see that there were plenty of moorings for visitors. On the previous occasion the basin

We tied up at Cambrian Wharf

had been packed with permanently moored boats and finding no room at all, we had moved on. There was only one other craft. Unfortunately, its engine was kept running for hours, presumably to charge the battery. It was noisy and smelly. People often do this outside our cottage which is worse for us as we cannot move away. This time we did; putting the breadth of the basin between us.

Locking up securely, (having stowed anything that was removable inside) we went into The Longboat for a beer. I glanced at the menu.

"'*Chips with Everything*'," observed Maurice. "D'you remember that play by Arnold Wesker we saw at the Rep.?"

"Mmn." I sighed. We had been subscribers to Birmingham Repertory Theatre in the past, never missing a production.

"Let's go and see what's on?" he suggested. But sadly, the main theatre was closed. I forget why.

"Never mind," I said, "let's go to the Art Gallery instead. That's free!" The City of Birmingham owns an impressive collection of pictures and the staff ring the changes quite often. I had spent many compulsory hours there when I was a student but I never tire of the place. Then, having been put in an artistic mood, we walked to New Street to see what was on at the upstairs gallery of the Royal Birmingham Society of Artists of which my father used to be a member. I am always on the lookout for new ideas and techniques. There are methods of painting now which had not been heard of when I was at art college.

A noisy evening and a comparatively quiet night was spent at Cambrian Wharf. The next morning we stocked up with groceries at the nearby V.G. stores; preparing to spend the weekend reacquainting ourselves with a portion of the B.C.N.

It took us just over an hour to get to Smethwick Junction where the New and Old Main Lines diverge. We turned right onto Brindley's earlier meandering route and mounted the three Smethwick locks. These have always had a poor reputation, mainly for vandalism, but apart from being stiff to work they seemed in fair condition. Then we were on the Smethwick summit where a chill March wind bit deep and swept icily through the concrete tube underneath the trunk road. At Spon Lane Junction, we bore left sticking to the Wolverhampton Level and crossing the New Main Line by Stewart Aqueduct. It was bitterly cold and sleeting. The protection offered by the M5 above was almost a relief although the wind still whistled in concert with the drumming of traffic overhead.

"I think the weather must always be like this here," I grumbled to Maurice. We had actually pulled in to the side on one occasion to give the dogs a run in the comparative shelter of the motorway. A big old boat slowed down alongside us; the steerer enquiring whether we could spare a tin of dog food for the greyhound he had just fished out of the cut!

This bit of the B.C.N. is complicated: so many junctions close to each other and short flights of locks going up and down between levels. We must have half a dozen (at least!) maps and guides of the area and none make it crystal clear. Three of them manage to split the most difficult part between two pages so that you have to turn back and forth to tell what's what. However, it is not half as difficult as you think when you are actually on the spot. My only advice is to stay in the middle of the channel. We have turned too sharply at many a junction in the past and ended up on a bank of silt.

A right hander at Oldbury Junction took us past the entrance to the Titford Canal. We had only been that way once (long before it hosted a National Rally) and the Pools were a tangled mess of old bedsteads and sunken hulks. Titford gets plenty of attention now so we did not spare any time but went on towards the next junction which was Brades Hall.

"Shall we have soup and sandwiches on the move?" I asked Maurice.

"Fine," he said. "It's pretty nippy up here. Perhaps it'll be better when we drop down onto the Birmingham level."

Shortly, we would have no alternative but to turn right off the Old Main Line as the way ahead was closed for maintenance. We just managed to finish our hasty lunch before Brades Hall locks, two of which are a staircase. Then we were on the Gower Branch which links the two main lines. It was a desolate place and did not feel any less cold. There were scores of men in hard hats with earth moving equipment squelching about in the mud. I believe the land has since been used for housing. I hope the residents have warm overcoats!

At Albion Junction we turned right again, and now we were on Telford's line going back towards Birmingham, running parallel with our outward trip on Brindley's.

Pudding Green Junction (to whet your appetite!) takes Wednesbury Old Canal towards Ryders Green Locks, the scene of several triumphant battles against weed and rubbish in the past. Today we passed it by, to bear right under the Stewart Aqueduct and hear the M5 thundering overhead once more. We considered tying up for the night near Galton Tunnel, another concrete tube, where we had moored happily in the past. But it had been summer then, the banks thick with rosebay willowherb and golden rod. Now it was less attractive.

"I'd sooner get back to Cambrian Wharf," I said, poised with the camera to photograph the graceful cast-iron Galton Aqueduct which carried the Engine Arm overhead.

"We should be there by tea-time," said Maurice. And so we were.

= 6 =

LAMB'S TALE

Rachel was the first of the ewes to drop her lambs. It was a cold and drizzly day a fortnight after Easter and unfortunately I was not there. Maurice spent a hectic and worrying morning trying to be shepherd and shop assistant at the same time.

"She was exhausted," he said to me when I got home, "and I didn't know what to do. I took the bag off one of them – she seemed too tired to lick it."

"Well done," I said. Sometimes lambs were born wrapped in the cawl and if it were not removed quickly from their faces they could not take a breath. Normally the ewe licked her lambs clean; it stimulated her milk to flow. "Where are they now?"

"In the pen," he said. "They're quite snug on the straw but you'd better go and have a look at them." I had been having lessons in lambing earlier that spring and was deemed by him to be an authority – which I was not. But I knew more than I had before which did not make me any happier. I was now aware of all the things which *can* go wrong instead of being sublimely ignorant.

Considering her ordeal, Rachel looked tolerably well and so did the larger of her two lambs. They were both coal black, the result of crossing a Jacob with a Suffolk. I was not certain that the little one had suckled, its tummy was still concave, so I fetched some ewe's first milk from the freezer and thawed it in the microwave. My intention was to tube-feed it to the lamb but the stuff was so thick that it clogged the tube.

"No good," I said regretfully, "it's like egg custard. Maybe the microwave cooked it. Anyway, both lambs are suckling now so I'll leave it. We may need the rest of the milk for one of the others." Secretly, I dreaded feeding a lamb by tube in spite of having done it once before (under supervision).

Yvonne's daughter, Carrie, was a professional shepherd. She travelled the country – and the world! – to work with sheep. At this time of year her job was to lamb flocks from Lands End to John o'Groats, often going back to the same farms from year to year. Carrie said she preferred the night shifts because then she was her own boss. I had asked if I could watch her at work when she lambed her father's flock and she said she would be glad of the company.

It was a cold morning as I tramped along the towpath and up the field in the grey dawn to Thrupp Grounds. When I got to the huge lambing shed, Carrie was not there so I just watched the ewes and got the feel of the place. A group of lambs in a corner pen were bleating plaintively, otherwise there was just the soft crunching of straw beneath hoofs and occasional baa-ing. Two new-born lambs were steaming in the chill air as their mother licked them.

"Hi," said Carrie, pushing the great door open just enough for her slight frame to slip through. "None of them were ready to lamb ten minutes ago so I nipped over to the house for a cuppa." She climbed onto a straw bale and scanned the barn. "There's one," she said, pointing at a ewe pawing the ground. "Come on, you do it."

"Me?" I asked, horrified. "How?"

She grinned as she grabbed one of the animal's back legs and toppled her over onto the straw. "Just push your hand in and get hold of the lamb. Roll your sleeves up first – it's a long way."

I did what she said. It was hot and slippery inside the ewe. Water-bags shifted as I tried to feel for feet, noses and ears.

"There'll be two, maybe three lambs", said Carrie. "Get hold of the front feet of the nearest one and pull gently. Put your fingers at the back of its skull at the same time to stop the head turning backwards."

The hard rim of the pelvis dug into my forearm as I followed her instructions. Suddenly the lamb slithered out and there was a sweet, antiseptic smell as a water-bag burst on the floor, soaking the knees of my trousers.

"Now clean its mouth of mucus," said Carrie, "and shove it under the ewe's nose. She'll be happy licking while you lamb the other one."

The first lamb lay limp for a minute or two, then wriggled in response to the licking and lifted its head. By the time I had the second one on the straw it was struggling to its feet.

"Check for a third," directed Carrie but I could not find one and neither could she.

I subsequently lambed three ewes but I still felt incompetent, failing to find the third triplet in the last one. Then I helped to feed some of the lambs with a bottle and we walked round all the pens to give each of the ewes with lambs a bunch of sweet hay and fresh water. By then, Carrie's shift was nearly over and she had her report to write up – like a night nurse going off duty – so I left her to it.

It was snowing lightly by the time I walked home, and very cold. I thought how much better it was for ewes to lamb in a cosy shed instead of a chilly field. One poor little creature that had been dropped in the open prematurely had been lying moribund under an infra-red lamp. This was another asset to lambing and one which we already possessed. All we need is a lambing shed, I thought.

A couple of days later I noticed a trail of afterbirth hanging from Mistake. I managed to pen her and had a closer look.

"She's either aborting or she's already done so," I said to Maurice in dismay. "Why, I wonder?"

"Stress," he suggested. "Remember how she got her horns entangled in the hay net the other morning? She may have been fighting to get free for some time before I found her."

Mistake seemed untroubled but I kept her penned so that I could keep an eye on her. Sure enough, she dropped a tiny grey foetus on the grass after a few hours and that was that.

"Bother!" I grumbled to Maurice. "We'd better dispense with hay-nets."

"I'll make a rack instead," he said. "Those horns of theirs are nothing but a nuisance."

I said nothing although I agreed. The choice of breed had been *my* idea because I wanted to spin the wool. But the horns made foot-trimming a hazardous business and they often got caught up in the hedge and broke off leaving a stump which bled profusely. And one of Mistake's lower horns had the habit of curling in an arc towards her cheek. When it started to dig in and cause her discomfort we had to hack-saw the end of it off. How she hated that!

My third trip to Thrupp Grounds was hectic and I learnt a lot. This time I waited until Maurice went to bed before crunching up the frosty field to the farm. I lambed four ewes in quick succession and at one point Carrie and I were kneeling side by side working on different animals. One old ewe was difficult; not very dilated and razor-sharp pelvic bones that were painful to me - heaven knows what they felt like to the lambs! Another lamb was presented abnormally, rump first, and had to be pushed back in and turned round. I managed this under Carrie's guidance. There was a beautiful lazy Suffolk who refused to help herself at all and one huge lamb that took all my strength to deliver.

"It's jolly hard work when you're not used to it," I said to Carrie. "Don't you get tired?"

"Not specially," she said. "This is the last lot, anyway. Just a few stragglers left."

I went once more but there was not much going on so I did not stay long. Carrie had been very patient but I guess she must have had enough of me by then. I just hoped that I did not have to put all her lessons into practice at one go.

Three weeks after Mistake aborted, Leah followed suit for no apparent reason.

"This is terrible!" I said to Maurice. "Perhaps it's a virus."

"Maybe we should inoculate them next year," he suggested.

"Perhaps." I was loth to get on that particular treadmill. It is one thing to dose your animals when they are ill but another to fill them up regularly with all sorts of medicaments that can enter the food chain. I hit on the cause subsequently, I think.

We had been short of grass in the spring and took advantage of an early flush of growth on the lawn; using an electric fence to keep the ewes off the rest of the garden. But the previous season I had treated the lawn with a product which has since been banned. It caused miscarriages in pregnant women who handled it.

"I bet that's it!" I said to Maurice. "No more lawn-care and no inoculations."

"If you say so."

"There's only Sooty left to go," I said after Rachel had lambed. "She looks enormous – it must be soon. D'you know, I saw two great crows pulling wool out of her fleece as she sat with the others. What cheek! She kept poking her horns back but they wouldn't budge. Eventually, she stood up, walked off and lay down facing the other way. They flew off then, beaks full of black wool. Why don't they take it off the hedge or the wire? Poor Sooty. She's got a bald patch now."

"Perhaps crows prefer black wool in their nests," said Maurice.

"Mmn. I wonder..."

Sooty chose to lamb on a balmy morning but things did not go well and I was glad of Carrie's tuition. I sat on a stump in the orchard watching the ewe struggle for a time. With our own flock, I prefer them to lamb naturally if they can. Obviously she could not. The question was – could I grab her leg and tumble her over like Carrie did? The ewe had the whole orchard to run around and I did not want her to try in the state she was in. I failed at the first attempt. Already the lamb's nose and one front foot were sticking out. The second time I succeeded. Here goes, I thought, trying to remember everything Carrie had said. Oh, Lord - it was one large lamb stuck fast in the pelvis. Why could she not have had two small lambs for her very first effort? Sooty gave a heave and the head was forced out. Its tongue was blue and the head started to swell.

With a mighty effort I got the poor little devil out of its prison; hoping to God that I had not cracked a rib on the pelvis in the process. I thought I had better make sure that there was no twin but there was not. Sooty refused to look at the lamb, let alone lick it. It was alive, at least, and bleated as soon as I had cleared its mouth. I carried it into the pen, pushing an exhausted ewe in front of me. She continued to reject the lamb; totally disinterested at first then actually butting it away whenever it started to nuzzle her for a drink.

After a few hours she began to lick it. I dare not interfere although I felt it needed more attention than that. The next morning, she had taken to it but it still looked hungry so I gave it some milk by tube.

"It looks very lethargic and weak in spite of its size," I told Maurice.

By the evening, Sooty looked much recovered but the lamb seemed no better and was breathing fast. I begged an antibiotic tablet from the farm in case it had an infection and fed it crushed in some ewe's milk.

She continued to reject the lamb

"I still haven't seen it suck," I said, worriedly.

And so it continued. I milked Sooty and tube-fed the lamb which grew bigger and heavier but wandered dejectedly after her around the orchard. Eventually, convinced it had pneumonia, I put it in the back of the jeep and headed for the vet. He confirmed it and administered an injection of penicillin.

The last day of April was dry and sunny with a cold wind. The lamb was still alive but looked no better. Neither did I.

"You coughed all night," said Maurice. "It's this standing about in the cold feeding that lamb."

"Yes. It would be worth it if it recovers but I doubt it. I'll take it along for another jab. It's weird that it can grow so fast and look so ill."

I had scarcely lifted the lamb out of the jeep on my return from the vet before it gave a last gasp and died. Tears pricked my eyelids.

"So sad," I sniffed. "I'd got fond of the little chap after working so hard to keep him going."

"At least Sooty's O.K." said Maurice. But she bleated pathetically for hours, finally jumping out of the pen and running dementedly round the orchard looking for her lamb. I could hear her cries after we had gone to bed and felt responsible for her misery. Eventually, I pulled a pillow over my head and slept.

= 7 =

THINGS THAT GO BUMP

The month of May can be one of the loveliest if you live beside a waterway. I went for a late afternoon walk along the Leicester Arm. The towpath was getting overgrown; blue bugle, white deadnettle, fools parsley, vetch in all shades of mauve from palest pinky-white to deep purple, dandelions and the ever-present nettle at its most vicious. Water forget-me-nots clothed the bank and red, pink and white campions glowed beneath the budding hawthorn hedge. The wind was roaring in the bursting leaves of sycamores and rippling across fields of barley. Oil-seed rape was as tall as me, garish yellow with a sickly-sweet scent. Standing at the edge of the field, I looked across the brilliance to a green meadow where bullocks lay in the lee of the hedge by the gated road.

On the main line, a pair of camping boats was moored against the meadow bank; children tumbling down the hill in play. Across the canal, the field sloping up to Thrupp Grounds was dotted with ewes and lambs and sprigged with fallen wool. The farmhouse, built of Northamptonshire stone, shone soft gold. Everything was rain-washed and sharply focused.

When I got back, trousers saturated by the dripping undergrowth, I learnt from a customer that there had been a drama at Lock Number 8.

"I'll take a look," I said to Maurice, "before I change my clothes."

At the bottom of the drained lock there was a sorry sight. A red and green narrow boat lay at an angle on its side, water lapping halfway up the cabin walls. The painted castles on the stern doors were just above the water-line. Bright signwriting stated that it came from Great Linford. It must have been heading that way.

"What happened?" I asked Brenda Walker from nearby Anchor Cottage Crafts. She told me that four boats had been in the lock together. This one had been alongside a similar boat and well forward in the lock. Its bow had caught on the gate as the water level dropped. No-one noticed and the stern went down and filled with water. I shuddered when I learnt that there had been a baby on board, strapped inside. It was rescued minutes before the vessel sank, apparently.

"It was the boat's maiden voyage," added Brenda sadly. "They'd just collected it to take to their home mooring."

"No one seemed to be doing anything to raise it," I said to Maurice on my return. "Someone told me that the Fire Brigade was called to pump it out but British Waterways refused to allow it. Insisted they'd do it themselves. The nearest pumps are in Rugby - Hillmorton presumably."

Maurice went down the flight to see if anything was happening after we had closed the shop for the day.

"It's been pumped out," he said when he got back, "by the Fire Brigade. The boat's now moored in the pound below. A damned shame – it's brand new."

"The Fire Brigade! Why not B.W.?"

"He grinned. "I guess they couldn't find anyone to man the pumps on a Sunday!"

A week later, a well-dressed gentleman came into the shop and stood diffidently at the back while I served some other customers.

"Are these Buckby Locks?" he asked, after buying something so trivial that I knew instantly that the purchase had not been his main purpose in coming inside.

"Yes." I nodded at the sign on the opposite side of the lock which said 'Buckby Top Lock' in peeling blue paint.

"Not Whilton Locks?"

"We...ell," I hesitated. "The bottom ones are often called that, although strictly speaking they're all part of the Buckby flight of seven. And Daventry District Council will persist in calling this one Norton Lock – which it clearly isn't!"

"Ah!" he said.

Pause.

"Do you have an open mind?" he said eventually.

"I like to think so," I said, trying to look encouraging.

"May I tell you something strange that happened to me twelve years ago."

"Fire away!" I said, intrigued.

"I was on a boat," he began, "delivering it, not holidaying. A friend was going to join me the next day to help me work up the flight but I was on my own that night." He paused again, looking embarrassed. "You'll never believe this."

"Try me," I said.

"It was dark," he went on, "when I tied up at the bottom of Buckby Locks – that's why I asked you what they were called." I nodded silently. "I went to bed after supper and fell asleep straightaway. The doors were locked, I'm absolutely certain." He halted and I held my breath. "During the night," he continued carefully, "a man with a beard tried to throttle me."

"What! Are you sure?"

"Yes. We struggled and in the end I pushed him off me and felt the beard."

"Then what?"

"He went away. I put on the light and he'd gone. I experienced a feeling of extreme cold – my teeth were chattering and I was icy. I got up and checked the doors. They were definitely locked. I was still shivering so I made myself some hot cocoa. After a bit, when I felt warmer, I went back to bed and tried to go to sleep. Again there was this sensation of great cold – and fear. More cocoa. It happened two or three times. At first light everything seemed to get back to normal. The cabin suddenly seemed warmer and my fear melted so I lay on the bunk and slept soundly until breakfast-time."

"Wow!" was all I could say.

He cleared his throat. "Today I found myself in the same district and decided to revisit the spot."

"Brave of you," I said. "Well, I *have* heard of some creepy happenings near the bottom of the flight but not that particular one. However, there's an old retired working boatman who lives down there. Henry Grantham will know about your bearded villain if anyone does. Tell him I sent you."

"I'll do that. Thanks for your help – and for not laughing at me."

Maurice and I chewed over the tale later that evening. Neither of us thought it was in the least amusing and I noticed him locking up particularly carefully before we went to bed. The next day I forgot about the ghost story because something else happened which drove it out of my head.

Maurice had just got back from the Cash and Carry and was busy unloading the jeep while I restocked the shelves, depleted after the weekend. Neither of us saw the start of the incident. Bystanders told us with relish.

Immediately above the lock the water is very deep to allow for the great gates to open outwards. It was at that precise spot that a woman in her late seventies fell into the canal. The boat on which she was travelling had just emerged from the full lock and had almost stopped; crew with ropes at the ready. Although the bollards positioned there are only intended for the use of boats waiting to enter the lock, many people use them as a convenient (for them) mooring. Just as the woman was stepping off the boat's counter onto the bank, the hem of her skirt got caught round the stud. The lock-keeper and his mate fished her out – very heavy, she was, so he said.

The first I knew about it was when a female off a converted working boat rushed into the shop, demanding a blanket. I provided a bath towel. Whereupon madam proceeded to undress the unfortunate old lady on the lockside! I stared out of the window in amazement, convinced that the victim would have preferred to take the three or four paces necessary to

down to thermal underwear

go into her own snug cabin (chimney smoking) and strip off in privacy. But Bossy-boots did not give her a chance to argue. Having forcibly peeled off all layers down to thermal underwear, which she mercifully left, she wrapped the soggy torso in my towel and gave the wrinkled shoulders a comforting squeeze. Then she thrust the wet clothes in a heap on the deck and strode away; feeling very virtuous, no doubt. I was left to wash the towel when it was finally returned, without much gratitude, by the steerer of the old girl's boat.

It seemed to be a good week for bodies falling in – though the second one was canine. This time, the lock was empty as a boat had recently gone down. The top gates have always been leaky and it gradually fills by itself when the bottom ones are shut.

A teenage girl walked past the window, a yellow labrador at her heels. She hopped up onto the lock-beam and crossed the chamber. The dog tentatively put his front paws on the beam, quickly withdrew them and backed away. The girl came back and seemed to be telling the animal not to be stupid, it was quite safe, *et cetera*. She grabbed him by the scruff of his neck and tried to drag him up onto the beam but he placed his plump bottom on the path and dug in all four paws. Irritated, she marched across the lock, calling his name.

"Use the bridge," I muttered ineffectually through the glass at her back view. "He'll fall in if you keep on so."

Having got to the other side, she stood whistling and calling until the animal's innate breeding overcame his fear and he decided to make a dash for it. But labradors are incapable of doing anything without wagging their long, strong tails. One clout of that muscular appendage against the iron railing thrust its owner off the beam and down into the abyss. The girl looked stricken, rushed to the lock-side, glanced down and then across at my window.

"Is he hurt?" I mouthed. She shook her head; making no attempt to rescue her pet. After another minute or so of trying to persuade the dog to jump out by himself (a matter of roughly nine feet from cill to lock-side) she came over and opened the shop door.

"I can't get him out," she said. "Can you do something?"

I was not keen on leaving the premises unattended. "Are you off a boat?" She nodded. "Well, fetch a boat-hook and pull the dog up the gate by his collar."

"He isn't wearing one – Mum says it makes a mark on his neck."

"Ah!" I put another option to her. "Open the bottom lock gate. You'll see some steps just the other side. Stand on the lowest step and call him – I bet he'll swim towards you and then you can fish him out easily." She looked doubtful.

"I'd better get Dad," she said, indicating a boat at the water-point nearby.

"A good idea," I replied.

The man abandoned the hose he was coiling and walked briskly towards the lock with his daughter, who pointed towards the steps. Her father shook his head.

At this point, curiosity got the better of me. I went outside and glanced into the lock. The dog was splashing about merrily in the slippery mire on the cill; yapping in the direction of his owners now and then. When he stood on his hind legs his front paws were nearly halfway up the gate. If he had had a strong collar on, it would have been a piece of cake. I looked across at the girl's father. He looked fairly fit.

"If you climb down onto the cill and heave him up to us, we can haul him out, I'm sure," I suggested.

He glanced down at his immaculate boating gear and gave no reply. Then he walked back along the path, opened the front gate of the lock-keeper's cottage and knocked on the door. The lock-keeper had a big heart. Within five minutes, he had clambered down into the lock chamber, gathered the hefty animal in his arms and climbed back out. The dog was covered in grey mud and green slime, some of which had been transferred to his rescuer.

The girl's eye caught mine. I gave her a thumbs up and escaped indoors hastily before I could be asked for another bath towel!

Just before closing time, I prepared to paint some canal ware. We were running short of enamel mugs in spite of the winter's work. I had also been commissioned to paint some 'personalised' ones emblazoned with the names of individual members of a boat's crew. I was first asked to do this by a cousin of mine. Wendy is an actress with a beautiful singing voice and she had just completed a run in the West End production of The Sound of Music in which Petula Clark starred. She gave Maurice and me complimentary tickets as a Christmas present which was lovely. When the show closed, Wendy gave each member of the cast one of my painted mugs decorated with roses around each person's name. After they were all finished, they made an impressive pyramid behind my work-table and brought in many orders.

As I unpacked a box of mugs, a late customer walked in. She leant on the wooden partition and watched me for a second before she spoke.

"Do you employ a professional to do the painting," she asked, "or do you do it yourself?" Ouch! She then went on to say that, of course, in the old days the boatmen painted with their fingers as brushes hadn't been invented when the canals were built. "I know it's true," she said, "because an old woman sitting beside the canal told me so."

"Really?" I said politely, wondering whether she had considered how the Old Masters executed their priceless works of art. I was reminded of an occasion on our second canal holiday ever. We had just crossed the Pontcysyllte Aqueduct in a hired boat when a very old man who had been sitting beside the basin at Trevor accosted us. 'I bet you don't know how the water stays in that thing?' he volunteered, pointing at the aqueduct. 'How does it?' asked Bruce. 'The trough's lined with Welsh flannel and black treacle', came the answer, 'and that's the truth.'

Yet another body plummeted downwards during May. It was human and landed with a thump on the fibre-glass roof of his own cruiser floating in the half-drained lock. Unfortunately, the man landed awkwardly and caught his foot on a cleat. The lock-keeper dashed into the shop and asked me to phone for an ambulance.

"His ankle's pouring blood," said he, "I guess he's torn an artery!"

"I'll come over," I said. "Tell him to raise his foot higher than his heart – I'll be there in two ticks." I ran upstairs and got some sterile dressings and bandages.

When I got to the cruiser, the man was sitting on the cabin floor with his foot propped up high against the door post. He had a greyish pallor and looked shaken.

"It's stopped bleeding," he told me.

"Good," I said. "Don't put your foot down for the moment. I'll put a sterile pad on the wound and a firm crêpe bandage." Then the lock-keeper and I eased the man onto a seat, propping up his injured leg. "Are your tetanus jabs up to date?" I asked. He shook his head dully. "Ask the doctor to give you a shot," I suggested. "There's lock-jaw in the soil round here."

"O.K." he said. "Thanks."

I found a blanket and he huddled into it. The lock-keeper stayed with him until the ambulance arrived and shortly afterwards popped his head round the door to say that the man had been taken to the casualty department in Rugby."

"What did the ambulance men say about his injury?" I asked.

"Nothing much, just that you'd made such a good job of bandaging it they'd leave it as it was. 'Fraid you can kiss goodbye to your bandage."

But he was wrong. The poor man hobbled in a few hours later, having been deposited by taxi from Rugby.

"Here's your bandage back," he said. "Sorry I haven't been able to wash it. Thanks ever so. And by the way – I got my tetanus jab."

"You're never going on with your holiday?"

"I'd like to – if I can persuade my brother to come and work the locks. I don't reckon on managing single-handed now!

"I should think not!" I said, laughing. "Take care."

A golden summery morning that did not last into the afternoon was typical of the Spring Bank Holiday. My father had a dictum that it was always fine on Good Friday and wet on Whit Monday. He was proved right even more frequently after Whitsun was abolished as a public holiday. Now it often rains, not only on the old feast day but the new one as well. Maybe someone up there is displeased by the re-arrangement!

I saw Henry Grantham approaching the shop, accompanied by a small Alsatian bitch which he ordered to sit alongside our 'dog-mooring' post.

"Hullo, Henry," I greeted him. "Baccy, is it?"

"That's right, me duck." He smiled broadly, showing a lot of gum and the stumps of one or two decrepit teeth. "Your chap come and asked me about his ghost." He opened the packet of tobacco and rubbed the strands between his fingers so that the scent of it pervaded the room. "I couldn't tell him nothing – not about *his* ghost, any road. I've never heard of no bearded fellow hereabouts. Not a real man nor a spook, neither."

"Oh!" I was disappointed. "I felt sure you'd know."

"I've seen 'em myself, mind you. Different ones."

"Where?" I asked him eagerly.

"At Whilton locks," he said, filling his pipe. "Years ago, it were, in the pub where The Locks is now. The Spotted Cow it were called.

The landlord and me was playing darts. It were after closing time and the landlord tell me 'e were just going to lock up. We carried on after. Then I saw a man standing between me and the dartboard. A big chap. I says to landlord, 'Jack – thought you said you was locking up?' 'I 'ave,' says Jack. 'Who's that, then?' I says. Jack turns and looks at the dartboard and sees 'im too. Before we gets near, dratted fellow vanishes."

"Whew!"

"True as I stand 'ere," said Henry. "Saw another, too."

"Where?"

"Stoke Bruerne. I were on the boats in them days. Two of us, with a motor and butty. Saw a woman in a long white nightgown sitting on the beam. It were cold and nearly dark. Six o'clock or thereabouts. I called my mate to take a look. 'Christ!' 'e says. 'That's me ma-in-law!' Then she disappears. We finishes the trip and goes back down with another load. My mate gets 'ome and finds his mother-in-law died at that exact time." He paused with his hand on the door. "Queer, aint it?"

= 8 =

IN BLACK AND WHITE

The heat wave which cannily delayed its arrival until the day *after* the bank holiday, stayed with us for a week and then abruptly departed. It was replaced by torrential showers.

"Flaming June," grumbled Maurice. "We'll never sell all that ice-cream."

"I hate ice-cream," I repeated sourly. He knew that I was not referring to eating it myself – in fact I have to restrain myself – but to selling it. We had constant aggravation from the wholesaler. Our orders were seldom correct. Sometimes I thought they must have hurled into the bags any old variety which happened to be kicking around the warehouse; hoping that no-one would check the delivery note. On one occasion I had loaded into the freezer the complete consignment for another shop before I noticed the name at the top of the computer print-out.

"Oh dear! Whatever shall I do," I wailed.

"Nothing," said Maurice firmly, splitting open a carton and quickly selling three ice lollies. "The delivery was as close to our order as it ever is."

"I'd better phone to say what's missing, at least." If that was not done, we would have to pay for what had not been received. "Continuous tone," I said, "have they changed their number again?" This happened so often we had begun to think it was a deliberate policy in order to side-step complaints!

Another irritant was the ice-cream freezer itself. Access to it was by two heavy glass panels on the top which were supposed to slide easily across each other. Due to a fault in design (had anyone actually designed them?), one panel fouled the other. The resultant 'klunk' jarred my shoulder sharply. At the end of a sunny, ice-cream-selling day I had to borrow the infra-red lamp from the day-old chicks or resort to smelly embrocation. At the close of the summer season, my over-developed right shoulder and upper arm muscle gave me a strange lop-sided appearance of which I was acutely conscious. I could not regret that the change in the weather cooled the market for ice-cream.

Rambling along the towpath, I thought that I had never seen the cow parsley so tall. A meagre mower's width had been cut, along which I forced my way, head ducked to avoid the creamy, moisture laden bower. Hawthorn twigs, heavy with saturated blossom, pushed out from the side to snag my clothes. It was hard to believe that the reservoirs had ever been empty.

By midsummer's day only one of our rose bushes, the old thornless 'Zéphirine Drouhin', was in bloom. 'What I choose to call a rose-garden' looked pathetic. Fat buds were rotting on lax stems. I had chosen these ancient varieties for their history, scent, colour and especially their form. Not, I admit, for their resistance to disease and our English weather. It is not an accident that the names of these old roses are Mediterranean. 'Souvenir de la Malmaison' for instance, dates from 1843 and should have large blooms which are full of petals, quartered, and constantly in flower. It has – sometimes.

'Madame Isaac Pereire' was another of my choices; a later developed rose, 1880. It should have large full flowers, quartered, of deep magenta pink. It does – sometimes.

However, there have been two resounding successes. One is a modern shrub rose which follows the form of the old ones. It is called 'Mary Rose' and I bought it because some of the proceeds went towards the fund to raise the wreck of the flag ship of Henry V111. Somehow, its heavy scented blooms surmount our wet and windy weather and it goes on flowering until the first frost. Its stems are sturdy and although its full, quartered face is vulnerable to rain, it survives all but the heaviest downpour. The second is a non recurrent variety called 'Complicata'. This is so vigorous and such a blaze of glory when it does flower that I forgive it its single surge of energy. I hack it down unmercifully each autumn but it takes off again every spring without taking umbrage in the slightest.

A third rose success which I almost forgot is 'Rosa Rugosa'. This cost us nothing because Maurice put a handful of rose hips in his pocket one day while he was waiting for a lock to fill. I stuck them in a pot of sand which I left in the garden shed during the winter to get thoroughly frosted. In the spring I squashed open the hips and sowed the seeds in a tray. To my pleased surprise, I ended up with dozens of tiny plants for which I had to find space in the garden. I popped them in wherever I could find a cranny against a fence or wall and they have flourished. All the bushes have turned out to be deep pink in various shades, strongly scented and perpetually flowering throughout the summer. When autumn comes, they produce fat, glowing red hips which hang on through the winter. It is then the real bonus is apparent. I have watched a yellow wagtail feasting off these rose-hips in January. He pecked and pecked at the squashy middle of the hip, swallowing busily. Now and again, he paused to regurgitate the seeds, having retained the pulp. Methodically, the bird worked his way steadily through all the hips on the bush in front of the parlour window before, I guess, moving on to another somewhere else in the garden.

I think it is a pity that some gardeners are quick to complete the autumn tidy-up of their patch. I suppose dead Michaelmas-daisies and suchlike are not particularly attractive in the garden but they do provide a natural food for wild birds.

We seemed to be having more problems with plant diseases than usual; rust put paid to the hollyhocks and infected the red-currants; black spot was usually troublesome on the shrub roses but this year attacked the modern hybrid teas as well; mildew was rife on almost everything. The only vegetables which looked really good were the brassicas and runner beans. I have got a fool-proof method with the latter.

First, I chit the beans by laying the seeds on moist kitchen paper in a plastic margarine container with a lid which is placed in the airing cupboard. After a few days, some of the beans start shooting out long white root tendrils. I pot each one as it chits because the roots grow so fast they get tangled and suffer damage when they are separated. As we do not heat our greenhouse, the pots sit on windowsills indoors until all danger of frost is past. With us, this is late May. Then they go into the greenhouse until mid June when I plant them out in the prepared bean bed. Maurice will have dug a trench and lined the base with layers of torn-up newspaper which he soaked thoroughly. Then he put in a layer of compost, shovelled the earth back in and erected the bean poles. We get such strong winds that a hefty post is needed at each end of the row and one in the middle. Cross-pollination is rarely a problem, even in dry weather. A hearty thwack on the poles at midday generally gets the pollen flying about. The only pest we have suffered of late is the rape weevil which gets inside the flower and eats its heart out. Last year it spoilt the first bean flowers but did not ruin the crop.

At the end of June, Maurice disposed of Gandalf. We were both sad about it and I am sure Maurice disliked doing it but Gandalf had got very bad-tempered with his hens lately. He chased them away from the food troughs and the scattered corn. Many of them looked pecked and woebegone. He no longer kept the flock together either, as they all went off in different directions leaving him alone guarding the feed shed.

That evening I watched them feeding without him and there is a definite pecking order which seemed to me to be colour related. 1: White hens. 2: Brown hens. 3: Marans (black and white) accompanied by our one remaining old Bantam (black and white). 4: Marans (dark brown and white).

With Gandalf out of the way, I released a mother hen and her five chicks into the orchard. Ever since she hatched them, they had been kept in a separate hen run. I also let out half a dozen Light Sussex young birds. Stephanie and I had driven over to Dorsington Manor near Stratford, back in May, and bought them as day-olds from The Domestic Fowl Trust.

We got rid of Leah too. She was in the peak of condition, having aborted early in pregnancy, and eating her head off. She had always been tricky and with no lambs to look after had become cunning as well as uncooperative. So we advertised her in the local paper and sold her to a man who wanted her as a present for his daughter. He did not wish to have the bother of getting her sheared so he was happy to wait until she had been done with the others, allowing me to keep the fleece. Nursing growing lambs takes such a lot out of a ewe that their fleeces are often thin and scruffy by shearing time. Leah's fleece was in first-rate condition and I looked forward to spinning it.

July was specially memorable to me because it was the month in which my first full-length piece of writing was published. I cannot describe adequately the thrill I felt when I saw the proofs and read my own words printed in black and white. The book had taken me a year to write – often while I was simultaneously minding the shop. The ideas buzzed about in my head all the time; when I was gardening, painting, cooking, vacuuming, walking, lying in bed (especially lying in bed) or in the bath. But actually getting those ideas down on paper in some sort of coherent order had to take place in front of a typewriter. So naturally enough, if I was clacking away within earshot of the shop bell, Maurice went off to do something useful outside.

I am a self-taught typist and make many mistakes; sometimes literally *painting* with Tippex! Any alteration which entailed retyping a whole page seemed a catastrophe. There must be many improvements I could have made to the finished product if it had not meant doing just that. Now that we have invested in an Amstrad PCW, I have no such excuse.

After writing preliminary letters to various publishers and sending them samples of the book (long before it was even half-finished!), we posted off the completed typescript to one of those who expressed interest. Thinking of the time and effort as well as reams of paper and spools of ribbon which I had spent, Maurice paid extra to send the parcel by a postal service known as 'compensation fee paid'.

my first full-length piece of writing

Ten days later half the script arrived back on the doorstep. Half! And of the half that was returned in a plastic G.P.O. bag, much was dog-eared and some positively chewed.

The question in my mind was whether or not the complete script had ever arrived at the publisher's. It was probably too much to hope that their delighted acceptance of my work had been lost together with the other half. Correct. A brief phone call established they had never received it. So then we put the wheels in motion to secure the compensation. This was surprisingly painless. We were given the maximum amount of compensation plus a letter of apology.

"Whew! Maurice stared at the cheque. "Not bad for an unpublished book!"

"A pound for every day I spent writing it," I said. "Thank goodness there's a duplicate. Some of that money can go towards getting some photocopies made and then I'll send it off again."

But before that happened, a publisher came to *me*, not to seek my literary work but to wholesale some of his own to our shop. Here was my opportunity – if only I could be brash enough to grab it! I am hopeless at selling myself.

Michael Pearson was promoting a new addition to his series of 'Canal Companions' – well-researched guide books for boaters, walkers and anyone interested in the waterways. Although we already stocked some of his publications, I had never met him. He had barely introduced himself when the shop was invaded by a boat load of school-children.

"Go ahead," he said. "I'll wait until you have a spare minute."

It is a convention (not always observed) in the retail trade that customers come before sales representatives. As I delved in the ice-cream freezer, I asked him whether he published anything else beside guide books. He said he did. I served the first batch of youngsters; plucking up courage to mention my own book and wishing Maurice was there to do it for me. Eventually I managed to introduce the subject and at Michael's request dashed into the other room to fetch the brief synopsis and a couple of extracts I had previously assembled to tempt publishers. These he scanned while I churned out more ice-cream to a second lot of children.

Then he nodded. "I like it," he said. "Can you let me have the complete script as soon as possible?"

"Of course," I said, trying to hide my glee. "I'd let you have it now but...I need to get a copy made first." I decided not to tell Michael about the compensation episode until after the contract was signed. He might have thought I did not need the money!

Things move at a peculiar pace in the world of publishing I discovered. They either romp away at breakneck speed or stand absolutely still. After the steady grind of writing the book, I found the waiting periods frustrating. Then I had to read the proofs in twenty-four hours over a bank holiday weekend! Not surprisingly, I missed a good many errors, some of which were mine and others the type-setter's. Altogether, ten months passed before publication day which happened to be Maurice's birthday.

"Let's have a party!" I suggested. "As well as friends and neighbours, we can ask everyone who is mentioned in the book."

"Heavens!" said Maurice, having dutifully read it. "In that case, it'll have to be a barbecue."

We were surprised at the number of people who accepted the invitation and at the number who ignored it. We also asked the media in the shape of local radio and newspapers. They all accepted; none of them turned up; most of them interviewed me subsequently. Even so, we had as large a gathering as we could easily cope with.

"What a mixed bunch!" I said, flicking through the list beforehand. "I do hope they talk to each other." I am not sure they did much of that, but I think everyone enjoyed themselves and they certainly tucked into the food with gusto. One couple brought all their relations. They apologised for leaving early on account of the little ones and each of them loaded a cardboard plate with kebabs, drumsticks, sausages, baked potatoes, onions, salad and anything else that was going, covered it with a napkin and took it away to eat at home!

It did not rain – quite. Or maybe it did – just. We had taken the precaution of hiring a small striped marquee (which Bruce said looked like a loo tent!) and a few people crammed into it right at the end of the evening. We had put the smaller barbecue under the cypress tree alongside the bed of herbs, which visitors picked to sprinkle on their food.

Most of the guests were dying to read what I had written about each of them, so we sold a lot of copies of 'Lock, Stock and Barrel' which is now almost out of print. All in all, it was a successful book-publishing party and I fell into bed that night in a blissful state of euphoria.

"Be prepared to get withdrawal symptoms," warned Maurice the next morning, as I tidied up my desk and threw away full notebooks and scraps of paper covered with scrawled memos to myself.

"I won't do that," I said blithely, searching out a fresh notebook.

"Why not?" He sounded suspicious.

"Because I've just had an idea..."

= 9 =

SUNNY SEPTEMBER

I first set eyes on Tiffany when she and her sister were standing on our doorstep, one of them holding a gift-wrapped bottle of wine.

"Mum and Dad sent this," said one of the girls, "to thank you for looking after our dog when he was hit by a car."

"Where do you live?" I asked, thanking them for the wine. The girls pointed across the main road towards a large house just visible in the lane.

"We moved in last week," explained Tiffany, observing my puzzled expression."

"If only I'd known," I said apologetically, "I wouldn't have taken him to the police station in Daventry. They filled in a form and would have kept him except that I insisted a vet should look at him. They don't deal with that, apparently, so I did. Had a bit of an argument there – but eventually the vet agreed to check him over and keep him under observation for a day or two in case there were internal injuries."

"There weren't," said Tiffany, "thank goodness."

"I'm so glad," I said. "He's a lovely dog and very obedient. He behaved beautifully in the car – sat on the floor in the front with his chin on the seat."

Shortly after that, Tiffany's mother became one of our few regular local customers. When the long school summer holidays loomed, we decided that our fortunes had prospered enough to advertise for seasonal help in the shop. The card had not been in the window for more than ten minutes before the job had been promised, in her absence, to Tiffany.

"She's leaving school this term," said Mrs Gregory, "and starting at Hull University in October. I know she's determined to do vacation work and this would suit her ever so well."

"Fine," said Maurice and I in unison.

"I'll tell Tiffany to come over and confirm it as soon as she gets home," said her mother. Which she did. Which, in its turn, explains how Maurice and I managed to have a fortnight aboard Warwickshire Lad in sunny September.

Stephanie had returned from Greece for good; arriving in August accompanied by two cats which went immediately into quarantine at vast expense. Without hesitation, she bought herself a tiny house in Long Buckby. Vine Cottage had once been a shoe-maker's dwelling and workshop. It needed a lot doing to it to make it habitable so Stephanie lived with us in the meantime and found herself a job as senior reporter on The Daventry Weekly Express. This, as you will see, also had a bearing on the outcome of our September cruise.

We delayed our departure until most schools had begun their autumn terms so that Tiffany would be able to cope single-handed. In fact, she had such a quick mind and so much energy that she could probably have managed by herself at any time. We had no qualms about leaving her in charge of the shop. The livestock would be Stephanie's responsibility.

The evenings were drawing in. 7.30 p.m. was the end of the boating day but it seemed quite late to us after a diet of winter holidays. We left home in warm sunshine on a Wednesday, hoping to avoid the weekend rush at Buckby and Stoke flights.

This was to be our first trip south since the route to London had been reopened. Warwickshire Lad may have motored through Blisworth Tunnel but its owners had not. We have always liked The Grand Union and looked forward to travelling along it again after such a long time.

The first day was spent happily cruising the eleven mile pound between Whilton and Gayton, meeting many people we knew or who recognised us. I had not realised that 'Lock, Stock & Barrel' would make us so well known. We stopped at Blisworth Tunnel Boats for fuel and lingered to have a coffee with the Gills. The ambient aroma was explained by a fractured pump-out tank in one of their boats. We pushed off hastily when we saw Dick and a mate emerging from the cabin, staggering beneath the split and stinking plastic coffin!

There were no free 'visitors' moorings' at Stoke Bruerne, which has a bustling waterways community and many full-length boats permanently moored there. So we went on down the flight and stopped at another of our favourite spots by one of the round-arched field bridges. On top of the hill, the chunky stone tower of Grafton Regis church was damson-coloured in the fading light.

Another mild morning with hazy sunshine took us through pleasant countryside disturbed only by the occasional noise of a train. The rural peace was shattered abruptly at Wolverton but this was nothing new. It is, after all, a railway town. At the sharp bend beneath the bridge which carries road and railway over the canal, we recalled capturing a tug, Vesta, which was adrift in the middle of the channel. She had been tied up on the non-towpath side – handy for her owners to catch a train at the nearby station, no doubt. Unfortunately, the vandals had found it just as easy to get at the tug and hack through the mooring ropes. We had difficulty in making her fast again with the sawn-off remnants.

Linford Wharf made an inviting place to tie up. There was only one other boat at the long jetty.

"We'd better give Tiffany a ring," said Maurice, "in case we don't come across another phone for ages. There's one in the village." It was our first brush with the phone card, I remember, but fortunately the nearby general stores had a note on the door telling us that they were obtainable within. Unfortunately, the shop was closed for lunch.

"Bother!" I said. "We'd better hang around until we can buy one – for all we know every single phone between here and London only takes phone cards." This was not true. The wretched card lasted us months, so rarely was it needed! Even now, a phone card only seems to be required at airports, railway stations – and Great Linford.

To fill in time, we sauntered past the ornamental lake and wandered round the old manorial buildings which Maurice photographed. I pencilled a quick sketch of the almshouses, intrigued by the curved gables and tall chimneys. An abundance of wild flowers flourished between the lichen-covered gravestones in the overgrown churchyard.

Shortly after we left Linford Wharf, having established that all was well at home, we approached a bend to find ourselves being waved down by someone who might have been in authority. It was not easy to be certain on account of his garb. He was wearing blue underpants (that was the clue) and standing on the back of a Waterways flat which was half-aground parallel with the bank. Beyond him, something which looked like the Loch Ness Monster was writhing about in the water. We hove to. I tried to see what was going on.

A second Waterways flat, complete with JCB on board, had sunk in the middle of the canal. A wet-suited diver was swimming around a blue flexible pipe which kept disappearing and then bobbing up again as if it had a life of its own. This was our monster. Blue Pants looked a worried man. He advised Maurice to give a sharp burst of the engine as we approached and then go into neutral as we went round the sunken portion of pipe.

"I suggest you get the diver out of the way first," said Maurice cheerfully.

We negotiated the obstacle without any trouble. As we rounded the bend, I looked back. The pipe had resumed its writhing, the diver his apparently aimless swimming and Blue Pants his anxious expression.

On our return a week later, the flat was still under water with the neck of the JCB sticking up like a drowned ostrich. Of Blue Pants, diver and Loch Ness Monster there was no sign.

We were no sooner out of sight of the sunken flat than a tall, bony man leapt out of the hedge bordering a quiet field. Middle-aged, with incongruously long hair pulled back into an elastic band, he looked extremely agitated. In one hand he held a plastic carrier-bag which probably contained his clothes as he was stark naked.

"A streaker!" I hissed at Maurice.

The man ran fast and easily ahead of our boat. Apart from one shifty glance at us as he landed on the towpath, he paid us no heed. Maurice accelerated slightly – out of devilment, I think – but the fellow was too quick for us. I saw his pallid buttocks disappear into the shadow of the next bridge like a pair of button mushrooms in the gloaming.

A second later, a fisherman with his wife and small daughter walked into view. We told them about the nude man and the fisherman left his womenfolk on the towpath while he went up onto the bridge to assess the scenery. He beckoned them to join him after a minute so I guess the coast was clear.

By then, we were alongside Newlands Park. This had been the site of the National Rally of Boats the previous month and a waterlogged venue *that* had turned out to be. Stephanie and I had squelched our way round the stands in spite of the deep straw laid by the organisers. Now, only white-painted numbers on the pilings indicated where the designated moorings had been. There were over five hundred. As soon as the park ended, Milton Keynes began – and never seemed to end. Row after row of new houses built of dark red brick and creosoted wood. Their gardens were miniscule. It came as a visual shock to us. We last cruised this way when

Milton Keynes only existed as a village surrounded by agricultural land.

Eventually we escaped from the uniformity and found ourselves in Fenny Stratford where we tied up short of the shallow lock. Opposite us, a home-made jetty with steps down to water level had been built at the end of someone's garden. It was probably intended for a canoe but all the ducks for miles around had congregated there; preening, snoozing and chuckling to each other. Nearby, at the end of a smooth lawn leading up to a whitewashed house, was a sign advertising Fenny Lodge Gallery. I found this irresistible so off we went to have a look round the gallery. One picture on display caught my fancy. It was a pen and wash drawing of Grafton Regis church from the canal bridge. To my delight, Maurice bought it secretly later and gave it to me for Christmas. On the way back we tried in vain to locate the exact spot from which the artist had painted her subject. Undoubtedly she had used artistic licence. I never dare do that. I reckon that it is permissible to move a tree or a stile for the sake of pictorial composition but something important like a church, a bridge or a hill should really stay where it is.

We had spent Friday night in the vicinity of Horton Lock. When I woke up, I could tell by a rheumaticky twinge that the weather was on the change. Mistakenly, I thought it was the discomfort which had woken me. Suddenly, there was a loud roar, short-lived but close by. It happened again and Maurice awoke.

"Whatever's that?" he exclaimed. The noise was repeated.

"I know you'll think I'm silly," I said sleepily, "but it sounds just like a hot air balloon being inflated."

Maurice got out of bed and went outside. "You're absolutely right," he said in an astonished voice. "It's just on the other side of this hedge."

I leapt out of bed and dragged on a track suit. Then I shot outside to take a look.

"Wonderful," I breathed, staring adoringly at the half-filled mass of brilliantly coloured nylon. It was puffing and straining at its tethers; dying to be up and away. "Get your camera," I instructed. "Quick! I'll try and sketch it but there may not be enough time."

I scribbled away with water-colour pencils as the balloon swelled above its basket. Suddenly it was in the air; rising effortlessly, the noise from the burners getting fainter. There was little wind although the clouds were menacing. The red and silver balloon shone like a bauble against the sullen sky.

Suddenly it was in the air

Eventually, I stopped gawping and got about the business of dressing and getting breakfast. We let go from our mooring with the balloon still high overhead. It just seemed to hang there and was visible for some hours. I think it was moving slower than we were. Finally, the sky cleared and a breeze developed; carrying the lovely object out of sight. But later, I managed to paint a picture from my sketch and Maurice's photographs. He gave the painting the appropriate title of 'Early Riser'.

I think there is only one other activity which competes with inland waterway cruising to provide a combination of exhilaration and tranquillity and that is hot air ballooning. I have only done it once – across the Masai Mara in Kenya – but how I would love to do it again! Every time I see a hot air balloon I gaze aloft enviously to try and recapture the experience.

Horton Lock was in our favour when we arrived at the bottom gates. We had seen a wide trip boat, loaded with passengers, go past us earlier in the opposite direction. Soon afterwards, we found the same boat on our tail coming up. It had a crew of two strong men as well as the steerer. Sometimes, in that situation, we are made to feel hassled. We frantically wind paddles and heave gates, thoroughly exhausting ourselves and end up at the top in a bad mood. Not this time. The crew came on ahead of their boat, helping us through so that it hastened them, chatting pleasantly although they must have been working harder than they would have had to do otherwise. After doing six locks in this manner, they waved us goodbye and turned towards Pitstone Wharf.

"I wish Marsworth reservoir was not just here," I complained, "where the locks are so close together. Then we could stop for a while and watch the birds."

"Hm." Maurice went ahead to set the next lock. It was too windy for me to leave the tiller, even for a second, to fetch my binoculars. There were hundreds of birds on the water but it was no good trying to identify them at this distance. A couple of 'twitchers' were very absorbed in focusing their telescope on something but I could not tell what it was. I did manage to see a pair of herons swooping among the gulls and that was about all!

"Shall we go down the Aylesbury Arm?" I suggested, after we had filled up with water at Marsworth. "Narrow locks would make a nice change and it's very pretty."

"Let's see how much time we've got on the way back," said Maurice. We wanted to get to London and venture up the Hertford Union – possibly some way along the Lee and Stort Navigation. We have army friends of long standing who live in Bengeo. They constantly try to persuade us to visit them by boat! We had attempted it once before but ran out of time before we got there. Now our calculations indicated that we might be successful.

Cruising plans can be thwarted in a trice. We had learnt as much early on in our boating career and this trip was to be no exception. On our fifth evening, we tied up in the gloom of the ancient trees originally planted for the Earls of Essex in Cassiobury Park. It can be a spooky place on a misty autumn evening. I tried not to think about the enormous negro who was supposed to have been able to leap the fourteen foot width of Cassiobury Bridge Lock which lay ahead. Legend says that he used to crash paddles down, slash ropes, thieve windlasses and generally put the fear of the Devil into boatmen. He was slain by one of them in the end – the weapon used was a windlass. A fitting judgement. There was a hollow tree, as the story goes, which revealed scores of rusty windlasses when it was felled not so long ago.

The next morning, with sunlight filtering through the yellowing leaves of the limes, the eerie atmosphere was somewhat dispelled. So I did not entirely jump out of my skin when a loud knock sounded on the cabin roof.

"You see who that is," I said nervously to Maurice.

"'Morning!" I heard him say amicably, so I bravely poked my head out. A couple of walkers plus dog were standing on the towpath.

"Are you Maurice and Shirley Ginger?" asked the man.

"Yes."

"Thought you might like to know that they're pulling the plug on Weedon aqueduct at the end of the week."

"What? Are you sure?"

"There was a paragraph about it in the Telegraph this morning," he said. "When we saw Warwickshire Lad tied up here, we wondered whether you knew."

"No," said Maurice. "Thanks very much. We'll have to revise our plans."

"I loved your book," said the woman shyly. "I hope you manage to get back in time."

"Thanks," I said. "You've been very helpful. 'Bye."

"Now I suppose we've got to turn round and go home," I said to Maurice after the friendly couple had gone. "Dianne Gill said the aqueduct was leaking but we all assumed that as it was so near the end of the season, there wouldn't be a stoppage until then."

"We've time to get to London and back, anyway," said Maurice. "If the worst comes to the worst, we'll have to leave the boat this side of the aqueduct until it's reopened."

"But that may take months! We need the boat as an extra bedroom at Christmas."

"The first thing to do is get to a phone and ring Tiffany." He yanked out the mooring spikes and shoved the stern out. "She can find out exactly what's going on."

At Cassiobury Bridge Lock, a loaded coal boat was going through ahead of us. The steerer had heard about the stoppage and told us that 'they were testing the aqueduct every eight hours'.

Then we came upon a blue narrow boat which must have broken down. It was being bow-hauled by its crew, ropes being lifted over and around irritated fishermen who were obviously taking part in a match. The steerer, a jolly chap with an oily face and curly black hair, asked us for a jump start. Our battery is not easily accessible, so we offered to tow them to a nearby boatyard instead. Curly Hair seemed to be the only one with a brain in his head. With the boat in tow, we cruised gently up to the marina and neatly cast them adrift alongside a grassy bank complete with vacant mooring posts. They managed to miss these altogether and ended up in a shambles among the moored boats!

It was late afternoon before we found a phone that worked. Tiffany said that there was conflicting information about the aqueduct. It was still open at the moment. Stephanie was on to the story, she said, and might be able to tell us more if we rang home one evening. We also phoned some friends who lived in Highgate; arranging to meet them for lunch in Camden the following day. That was as far as we felt we could go and still have a chance of getting back across the aqueduct.

On we went to Bulls Bridge Junction where we turned left off the main line onto the Paddington Arm. A few minutes later we found a Thames Barge loose across the canal. There were a number of others tied up near Southall gas works. It took a lot of effort to shift it out of the way. Maurice pushed and shoved with the long shaft but all that happened was that our boat went backwards while the barge stayed still. Finally, by dint of throttling up and saying my prayers, we slid through a narrow gap. The barge swung out again straight away, of course. We looked around for anyone who might have been responsible for the barges but there was not a soul to be seen. We had the same problem in reverse on the way back.

It is not easy to find pleasant, quiet moorings in London, so we stopped overnight at a place which Maurice remembered – he is good at that. On the chart it is called Horsenden Hill. We actually picked the boundary between a public and a private golf course, reckoning that as it was no-man's land we would not be disturbed. We were not – except by a pack of youngsters who rapped on the window to ask if they could use our loo!

At Kensal Green the next morning, we paused briefly. Maurice held the mooring ropes while I nipped up onto the bridge and round the corner. I was crossing my fingers that a small stores we remembered from years before was still there. We had discovered it on the Nicholas cruise when we explored Kensal Green cemetery.

Incidentally, if you have never been there, I can recommend a visit. It is the cemetery you always see on the television when there is a burial scene. Once you know it, you will recognise it instantly on the screen. There are huge family vaults, memorial arches, sarcophagi, obelisks and hundreds of ornamental headstones, some adorned with a likeness of the incumbent. The whole place covers a vast area and many famous people lie there. It even has its own access to the canal, where coffins were off-loaded from funeral barges. We did not discover that until later.

Yes, the corner shop still existed and had expanded its merchandise to include some rather strange wares. Probably it had changed hands. However, fresh milk was still available and that was what I wanted. So in a few minutes I was back on board and we were chugging along between the graveyard and Wormwood Scrubs.

One of the gas-holders between the prison and the towpath is Victorian. It is decorated with delicate cast-iron, like a park bandstand, in contrast with the stark lines of its neighbour. Both had been freshly painted white, striking against the deep blue sky.

At Little Venice, we stopped to fill up with water and make use of the sani-station so that Warwickshire Lad was all tidy to receive visitors. All the houseboats seemed deserted. I suppose the people who lived on them were out at work. The sharp bend at Paddington Stop took us by surprise. There, we had the first of several contretemps with a trip boat. This one was creaming out of the pool behind Browning Island and looked as if it were about to sink us rather than slacken speed. Perhaps we were in the wrong? The steerer did not give us time to discover our error before he motored under the bridge through which we had just emerged, to our relief.

"A bit of a contrast with the lovely chaps at Pitstone," I said acidly.

"This is London," said Maurice drily. "We'll have to watch out."

Now we were on the Regent's Canal and approaching Maida Hill tunnel. Sunshine dappled the water, sliding over the roofs of elegant Regency houses and through the branches of plane trees flanking the road on either side. Occasionally, a leaf the size of a tea plate wafted down onto the cabin top. Private boats occupied every inch of canal bank but we never saw one on the move while we were there. Just short of the tunnel, a scruffy seventy-footer called Kew was sticking out into the channel with insufficient room for us to pass. I steered and Maurice took the short shaft to push it over, thinking it must have come adrift at one end.

It would not budge. This was not surprising as there were two propane and two butane gas cylinders balanced on the edge of the counter. A man was in the depths of the engine. He did not speak or make any move to help, neither did his long-haired, long-skirted woman. We scraped through, no thanks to them. I magnanimously pointed out that there was a wide waterbus behind us. The female woke up slightly and pushed the boat round to the side very slowly.

We went through the tunnel with the waterbus hot on our heels. The driver signalled that we were not going fast enough, so we clung to the wall alongside the zoo to allow him to go in front. Then we rocked along in his wash and tied up gratefully next to the towpath above Hampstead Road lock.

"Whew!" I said. "It's just as well that Maida is a short tunnel and you can see the other end. I'd hate to meet one of those fellows going the opposite way!"

"It's a bit stressful," agreed Maurice, glancing at a passing trip boat which had just come up the lock.

We were having a therapeutic gin and tonic when our friends joined us on Warwickshire Lad. Then we all strolled along to Le Routier and found a table in the window overlooking the canal. A community boat laden with handicapped people accompanied by their helper entered the lock as we waited for our meal. Our friends, both medics, were interested in the concept of boating for the handicapped. We all watched idly as we talked. The vessel was being steered by a professional boatman who left the helper to work the lock. I had no sooner begun to tuck into cabbage leaves stuffed with duck in a dill sauce than Maurice pushed his chair back.

"I'm going to have to do something!" he said. "It's five minutes since that fellow raised the bottom paddles and the top ones are still wide open!" He went out and spoke to the helper who rushed about in anguish, dropping paddles and shouting explanations to the steerer. Then the trip boat we had seen go past us, reappeared. The steerer of the community boat leapt onto the bank, castigating the trip operator for leaving the top paddles open. I thought they would come to blows but the helper intervened. Eventually, peace reigned. The community boat departed and the trip boat went down the lock after it. Guess what? The operator left the bottom gates and paddles open, all handy for his return!

On reflection, I would not be happy with my boat permanently moored at Maida Vale. I should think the water level must be rather unpredictable.

After lunch, we investigated the craft 'village'. I bought a weird pot and two wooden cat brooches for Stephanie and Tiffany. We saw our friends off at the tube station before doing the rest of our shopping. Everything we wanted was to be had except a pepper mill. There was a superlative fishmonger which is a rarity.

It was early evening before we left. All the animals in the zoo had vanished indoors. As there were no locks to negotiate, we kept going after dusk fell and managed to make it back to Horsenden Hill in the dark. While I prepared supper, Maurice tramped round the deserted golf course to telephone Stephanie.

"Weedon aqueduct is going to be shut first thing on Monday," he told me on his return, "either until further notice or for six to eight weeks – take your pick! They won't know until they drain it. Stephanie has booked us a mooring at Stowe Hill Wharf if we don't make it across. She's got a front page story out of it which sounds ominous."

"Blasted media!" I said in disgust. "Even if it *is* our daughter. Why do they have to blow everything up?"

"We should get back in time," reassured Maurice, "without hurrying unduly. But there'll be no lying abed in the mornings," he warned.

"O.K." I sighed. "Who wants to be lazy on holiday, anyway? On one condition, though."

"What?"

"That we don't cut our holiday short because we happen to have got home early. We can pop in and say hullo to Tiffany and go on up the Leicester Arm for three or four days."

"All being well," he said, in his usual uncompromising way.

In the rosy sunshine of Sunday evening, we motored across the aqueduct. Stop planks and heavy machinery had already been assembled on the towpath.

"Pools on the road terrifying the inhabitants of Lower Weedon!" I said scathingly as I looked over the parapet. "There've been puddles down there on the road ever since I can remember."

They were there long after the aqueduct was repaired, too. It turned out to be blocked drains!

= 10 =

FLOTSAM & JETSAM

One week into October and storm clouds gathered and burst. Added to the stoppage at Weedon, this meant that scarcely anyone crossed the shop threshold. Gales and rain battered the garden. Windfalls would have littered the orchard if it had not been for the sheep clearing them up. It was a wonder that the animals did not get bloat but they seemed to thrive on apples. They ate the fallen leaves too. We grumbled about their greediness over the fruit but at least the ground looked tidy.

Only a few late apples lingered on the trees when the ewes went off to be tupped. We had found a Jacob ram at last, in the nearby village of Welton. It was an easy matter to pen them and dip their feet in a formalin footbath before they left. The difficulty was in loading them into our purpose-built trailer. Sooty escaped into the garden and we had to come back for her later. It was so dark by the time we released her into the field that she could not find the others at first and dashed about in a panic. It was snowing fitfully when we left, and chilly.

"I hope they don't get overheated when the ram gets after them," I said to Maurice. "It's a pity we couldn't have taken them over earlier."

Rachel's ram lamb was making a fuss when we got back; running up and down and bleating. We should have arranged it so that there were two lambs left but it never occurred to us. One on its own gets lonely.

In spite of the cold, four of the Light Sussex birds insisted on roosting at night high in the apple tree near the gate. The old bantam taught them this trick when the nights were warm. Now it had turned cold, she went indoors but the others stayed aloft. Several times I climbed a ladder at dusk, picked them off the branch, one by one, and shoved them into the henhouse. When I got bored with that, I tried hooking them off the branch with the shepherd's crook but they clung fast. The potential danger was at dawn – the fox would quite likely be lying in wait at the foot of the tree for them to drop at his feet.

Towards the end of the month, the aqueduct was opened to boat traffic. Although the work was finished on schedule, the through route was clear for only a few days. Maintenance restrictions then came into force. I watched British Waterways putting in the stop planks above Buckby Top Lock. It cannot have been an easy task as it took eight men the best part of a day. Then they surrounded the empty chamber with chestnut paling, fluorescent tapes and several 'Danger! Work in Progress!' notices although I do not remember any taking place.

We had hoped to have a proper lambing shed available for the ewes by the coming spring. A timber stable with two doors; one leading to the orchard and a second into an open-fronted field shelter seemed the best plan. If the field shelter had a five-barred gate opening onto the drive, it would serve as a place for sheep husbandry like shearing and foot-trimming as well as a useful store for logs, garden machinery, bicycles and the jeep. We ordered the structure well in advance from a firm in Banbury who promised no delay as soon as a concrete base had been laid by a local builder. That proved to be the snag. The winter had been comparatively mild until the end of January. Maurice nagged the builder, off and on, but he did not show up. I got more and more irritated by the unnecessary delay, Eventually, he undertook to come in the first week of February. I was not in the least surprised when the ground froze like iron two days before. This was followed by snow and more frost. So that was that until March.

At last the weather relented. The sun shone feebly and the temperature rose enough to thaw the canal. Water filmed the ice. A patch of visible grass round the cypress tree began to spread. But the frozen earth was unable to absorb the melting surface water which collected in puddles at the edge of the borders and on the drive. The month went out like the proverbial lion; smashing a large pane of glass in the greenhouse and bringing down a lilac tree across the towpath. April coldly entered. By the tenth, the last of the ewes had lambed. (The base for the lambing shed was completed the previous day.) We had lost one ewe lamb which arrived prematurely. I might have saved it if we had had the proper facilities – who knows?

Because our land slopes in two directions, there had been a fair amount of earth moving necessary to make the ground level for the base. We had asked the builder to spread the spoil in a long bank sloping up to the hedge. It was to be part of our 'wild garden'.

"What a dreadful mess!" said Maurice when all the workmen had departed. To the rear of the lambing shed, where once there had been springy turf, was a quagmire. Between the spinney and the orchard, a slag-heap of subsoil and stones towered in front of the hedge. In front of this, the area we called 'the sheep lawn' (it was nibbled not mown) had been disfigured by two deep ruts. Having carefully driven his dumper truck up and over the pile of spoil on every trip except the last, these ugly furrows had been the truck driver's parting salute! They took ages to obliterate because the weight of the vehicle had impacted the earth, causing them to act as storm drains in wet weather.

Maurice attacked the spoil heap with the cultivator but it was too tacky. There was nothing else to do but shift it with shovels by hand. When it looked more like a bank than a pyramid, we let it settle for a week before trying the cultivator again with more success. Then I spent all my efforts in hoeing and raking; trying to get the stuff to resemble a fine tilth. Being sterile subsoil and lacking humus, it was hopeless. As peat is a finite resource, I have stopped using it as a soil conditioner so I bought several bags of forest bark instead. It was expensive and went nowhere. Anything we could think of that would help – grass mowings, leaf mould, chopped straw, sawdust – was sprinkled on the bank and raked in.

"It'll be years before it's anything but an eyesore," said Maurice despondently.

"It jolly well won't!" I answered obstinately, wondering what else I could do to improve matters. "I know – worms!" I turned over the compost in the bin and extracted hundreds of tiny red worms which I 'planted' in pockets of rich soil placed in strategic places all over the bank. We did not have enough compost to spare from the vegetable garden and in any case, it would encourage weeds at the expense of wild flowers.

Grass seed was next on the agenda. Rye grass may be adequate for lawns but not for a wild garden. I wanted a wide mixture of bents and fescues which would seed readily and also make sweet hay. It costs a bit more but looks so pretty when all the delicate seed heads nod in the breeze. I also sowed packets and packets of different wild flowers which was an utter waste of money. Hardly any of them germinated, and of those that did, few set seed. But now that several inches of top-soil have developed, several species are colonising the bank uninvited. Primroses are doing well. Also bluebells, snowdrops, dog-daisies, evening primrose and many common wayside flowers.

"I've got to hand it to you," admitted Maurice before the summer was out, "the bank looks quite presentable from a distance."

It was mid May before all this work, as well as the spring sowing of the vegetable garden, was done. Suddenly, thanks to Stephanie, we had the chance of a mini-cruise.

"Four days," said Maurice as we let go from Buckby Wharf on a dryish day with a moist west wind. "Where shall we go?"

"The Ashby?" I suggested. "As far as Stoke Golding."

"How about Coventry? We've never gone in to the basin itself, which is where the Coventry Canal begins. I think we ought."

I wrinkled my nose. "Must we?"

"Let's see how we feel when we get to Hawkesbury," he said blandly. I knew that meant we were going to Coventry.

Spring had obviously arrived late; the banks of the Oxford Canal were rimmed with shiny yellow celandines and mauve cuckoo pint, although the distinctive call of their namesake was noticeably absent. Beyond Harborough Magna, the cutting was thickly lined with frosty-white blooms of blackthorn which normally flowers in March. The meadows were fringed with mats of cowslips. How I longed for some on the raw bank at home but I know it is wrong to dig flowers from the wild, so I refrained. There were moorhens sitting on nests precariously balanced on overhanging branches close to the water. They always hopped off the nest and swam away as we approached – acting as a decoy, I suppose – exposing fawn, speckled eggs. In another wooded cutting near Brinklow, I saw a fat water vole perched on a thin twig above the water. I thought it was a bird at first and wondered why it did not fly off. It was so insecure that it dared not move when we passed close by but glared balefully sideways at us. I saw it fall with a plop a minute later, though.

Hawkesbury Junction marks the northern end of the Oxford Canal. We chugged slowly past a loaded coal boat and exchanged a word or two with John and Madeleine Forth. They promised to fill up our bunker at home on their next trip south.

"Summer prices!" called Madeleine, as we drew away. She was busy feeding a beautiful black lurcher with the apt name of Slack.

Then we were through the shallow stop-lock, under the bridge and turning left towards the city of Coventry, as I knew we would. At Longford Bridge we stopped to phone Stephanie and do some shopping. The traffic was dense but almost everything we needed was available. We discovered a real-ale off licence called The Grape and the Grain where Maurice bought four pints of Hook Norton, one of our favourites.

the shallow stop-lock

I would like to sing the praises of the first five and a half miles of the Coventry Canal, but on the strength of that one visit I cannot bring myself to do so. I know the Coventry Canal Society work very hard on the section but it must be a thankless task. For rubbish, it takes some beating. Much of it had accumulated at the sharp bends. We had to put the gear into neutral and drift through the mass of half submerged polythene and other trash. This lost us steerage way to negotiate the bends. It would not have mattered much if there had been nothing coming the other way but quite often there was! If it were not for the hire boats regularly coming out from Swan Lane Wharf, I guess that stretch would clog up completely. The sharp bend after the boatyard was by far the worst. However, we soldiered on; intending to tie up in the heart of Coventry overnight.

"It sounds quite pleasant," I said, perusing the guide book. "There's a large basin surrounded by old wooden warehouses and only a spit from the cathedral. We could visit it tomorrow, if you like? It says here that at the start of the canal there is a stretch of surprisingly clean water."

"Huh!" Maurice went astern to dislodge a baulk of timber which straddled the stem. "I'll believe it when I see it."

The boat crept round the last bend. In front of us, the basin of (presumably) crystal-clear water was obscured by a fretwork of rusty scaffolding. The old wooden warehouses on the left were apparently being developed. The basin itself appeared to be divided into two arms by a peninsula which jutted towards us and tapered to a point close to the scaffolding. One arm was obstructed by the work in progress, the other was crammed full of deserted canal craft of one sort or another. The refuse disposal, sani-station and water point were inaccessible – also the shop and information centre, both of which were closed. It was very unwelcoming and I felt deflated. There is something about battling one's way down an underused waterway which makes one expect some sort of triumph at the end. Unreasonably, I suppose. The end of the Slough Arm presented a similar anti-climax although in that case we had not been led to believe that it would not. On that occasion, I recall that we passed an inspection launch travelling the other way. It was loaded with Waterways officials, one of whom had his nose in Nicholson's Ordnance Survey Guide to the Waterways. Maybe they were afraid of getting lost!

I hopped up on the roof to see whether the cathedral was visible over the high brick wall flanking the road and caught a quick glimpse. Maurice struggled to keep the boat clear of the scaffolding and the unfriendly metal edge of the peninsula. Eventually, he had Warwickshire Lad turned round and facing the way we had come.

"I've gone off the idea," I said morosely.

"Back?" he asked. "It's only a quarter to six."

I nodded and we set off through the debris for Hawkesbury, where we tied up for the night.

The next morning we woke to a changeable sort of day with a chill wind. I did not feel sorry to leave Hawkesbury which had quite altered since the site of the Central Electricity Generating Board had been turned into a vast noisy rubbish tip. Unfortunately, the engine would not start and inexplicably flattened the battery.

"The lights were bright enough yesterday evening," I said.

Maurice grunted his annoyance. "We never have all systems going at the same time, blast it!"

Eventually he managed to get us started. I did not like to mention that the submersible pump of the shower had gone phut as well. That would best be left for another occasion, I thought, mopping up the soapy water with a cloth when he was looking the other way.

As we retraced our route towards Stretton Stop, we tried with some success to see the line of the old Oxford Canal before Telford straightened out the loops. At Rose Narrowboats we stopped to get a replacement glass for our little paraffin lamp and a cowl to keep the rain out of the chimney when the stove is burning. When it is not in use, we have an upside-down stoneware dog's bowl which may look odd but serves the purpose. Then I weakened and bought a lithograph which I had been coveting for several years. It is numbered ninety-three out of a limited edition of a hundred, so it was as well that I had delayed no longer!

Cast-iron bridges made by Horsley Ironworks are photogenic and there are several between Stretton and Hillmorton. Maurice got out his camera but the results were disappointing as the light was dull. Not only that, the span across the overgrown Brinklow Arm had been painted a nasty blue. Almost immediately, the icy wind turned into a bitter hailstorm accompanied by lightning and thunder. The Fennis Field Arm bridge was still rusty black and looked spooky in the gloom.

We locked up Hillmorton in cold rain; my memories of these locks had all been of good weather – not any more. The sun had been shining there on our way down. It was hard to credit that we had stopped for me to sketch the skeleton of an abandoned boat below the bottom lock; sharp shadows picking out the bleached ribs.

Rain turned again to hail, clattering onto the cabin top and bouncing into the water with a thousand tiny plops.

"There's not a lot of pleasure to be got from cruising in these conditions," said Maurice, as we motored beneath Crick Road bridge. "Shall we call it a day?"

"It's very early to stop," I said doubtfully. There was an empty mooring alongside The Old Royal Oak which did look inviting though. "Yes!" I said suddenly as the hail doubled its ferocity. I jumped onto the wharf, hailstones crunching underfoot, and pulled on the rope with numb fingers. A good book beside the cosy stove was infinitely more attractive.

= 11 =

BLOOMING LOVELY

Chelsea Flower Show in the pouring rain has a lot to offer although it did not take me more than five minutes to realise that I was wearing the wrong footgear. We had caught the first train from Long Buckby hours before. The early morning had been promising and I settled on a pair of smartish sandals which would carry me comfortably along the seemingly endless paths of the Royal Hospital gardens. One look at the morass inside the main gate made me realise my mistake.

"Boots," I said firmly to Maurice. "Let's head for the trade stands first." I had visited Chelsea many times so I knew my way around. I bought a pair of short green gumboots with which I immediately replaced my sandals, to the salesman's amusement. They may have looked incongruous with the rest of my outfit but a lot of other folk glanced at them enviously, I noticed. Having got Maurice (who was new to Chelsea) in the vicinity of the trade stands, it was difficult to drag him away. By the time I did, he had ordered an ascender barrow – for carting bales of hay and straw – and a machine for munching up prunings to make compost. I managed to prevent him buying an expensive cold frame as we already had two, although they did not open and close automatically as this one was alleged to do.

"We've got a gadget for the greenhouse which is supposed to do that," I argued, "and it's never worked properly."

The heavens opened about then and everyone else made a dash for the vast marquee which was soon crammed with people. Maurice had brought an umbrella so we walked over to the display gardens in the open on the far side. On previous occasions, people have been wedged yards deep in front of me and I had never managed more than a glimpse between heads. This time we lingered in front of each garden; noting different plants: jotting down ideas; photographing the layouts from various angles. There was hardly another soul about.

We even had time to study the entries for a competition run by a national newspaper and place our vote in the box. I find the individual gardens more interesting than the exhibits in the marquee although the latter can be spectacular. I genuinely try to appreciate plants in bloom without coveting them but nearly always succumb to temptation in the end. This time it was clematis and astilbe which captured my fancy and my money.

The National Farmers Union always have an eye-catching stand and this year was no exception. On top of a red wagon stood a little house entirely made of perfect garden produce arranged in slabs of brilliant colour – reds, greens, purples and creamy white. The quality of the vegetables made *me* green with envy, although as Maurice pointed out, they were probably loaded with chemicals.

The only exhibit which was easily matched by our own garden was the 'Which on Weeds' display by the consumer magazine. We scrutinised it carefully and reckoned that we grow every single weed shown in large numbers!

A visit to Chelsea Flower Show has a dual effect on me. It makes me despondent when I look at my own garden; comparing its shortcomings with the perfection I have just seen. It also inspires me to work harder to improve it. Fortunately, the second effect is more long-lasting than the first.

I did not get much chance to put my new-found enthusiasm into practice straightaway as the schools broke up for half term and we were too busy in the shop. There were also two orders for large Buckby cans to be painted with the boats' names round the middle. I always enjoyed doing those. I still get a thrill when we are travelling on the waterways and I spy one of my cans on the roof of a boat. I always recognise my own painting instantly - and that of most of my competitors. Sometimes a watercan is sold with the boat and the new owner may not know who painted his can – but I could probably tell him!

Another interesting commission was to paint an enormous old paraffin lamp which had been in use on a steam train engine called The City of Truro, after which the customer had named his boat. He had already given the lamp a background coat of dark green. It looked splendid when it was smothered in roses and daisies; the name painted round the base in ivory, shaded with orange and red.

"If you're planning to put it on the foredeck," I said to the delighted owner when he collected it, "you'll need a fair bit of ballast at the stern to stop the boat nose-diving!"

He laughed. "We'll probably keep it at home."

The City of Truro

The end of the month marked the publication of my second book which was a beginner's guide to the technique of narrow boat painting. So many customers had asked me how it was done; wanting to try their hand at it, that I felt there was a slot in the market provided we could keep the price low. This idea had germinated almost as soon as 'Lock, Stock & Barrel' was on the shelves.

"It must be in colour," I insisted when Maurice and I were initially discussing the project. "And I've got to assume that the reader is an absolute novice at painting anything. Everything must be spelt out from first principles to a finished castle scene."

"Lettering?" he asked.

"Hm." I considered for a moment. "I don't think so. Sign-writing is a different kettle of fish altogether. In any case, it's the roses and castles that excite so many people. Only boat-owners wanting to do a repaint are interested in lettering and therefore the demand would be limited."

I decided that the colour illustrations should feature a wooden cabin stool. A castle scene would be painted on the seat, roses on the sides, daisies front and back, decorative borders all around. At each stage in the painting sequence I paused, so that Stephanie (who is no mean photographer) could capture my work on film. When that was done and the colour slides developed, I elaborated by means of pen and ink drawings. Letter-press, though important, was kept to a minimum. I believe in the old adage – 'one picture tells a thousand words'.

The next task was to decide on a format and find an appropriate printer. I had bought a Wisley Handbook from the Royal Horticultural stand at Chelsea and I used this as a model. The printer's address was on the back cover so off we went to Banbury during the winter to see him. By good fortune, the printer also specialised in fine art reproductions and was happy with Stephanie's efforts. In publishing the book ourselves, we realised how much is involved in getting a manuscript and illustrations licked into the shape of a finished volume – however slim. And slimness (or thickness), we learnt, is what governs the price of the finished product. That and the colour illustrations which turned out to be expensive but, in my view, essential.

At last it was ready. In order to have what is called 'ecomomies of scale', we had to have an initial print run of three thousand. Gulp! And the printer wanted a thousand pounds in advance. I remember him telephoning me when Maurice was out, to say that they were just about to start the run and would I please confirm that we wanted three thousand copies. I felt distinctly queasy and had to sit down when he had rung off. What if nobody bought it? We needed to sell fifteen hundred to break even. Did fifteen hundred people really want to know how to paint roses and castles? The answer, ultimately, was yes, yes, and yes again. We were on to a winner and six months later we knew it. Apart from selling the book across our own counter, we were selling copies to almost every shop on the waterways system as well as museums, canal societies and centres for adult education. This was largely due to a friend of ours, Barry Whitehouse, who agreed to act as our distributor. He shifted hundreds of copies before he retired and then Toby Bryant kindly took over.

Shortly after the publication of 'Simple Steps to Roses & Castles', I was invited to be interviewed by Radio Northampton as part of a series based on the waterways, mainly the River Nene. The radio team had borrowed a boat from Dianne and Dick Gill and were broadcasting daily as they cruised down-river, mooring at strategic places. It was a damp, blustery day when I drove to Wadenhoe, near Oundle, to meet them. My interview took place on board Tardebigge Tunnel which was moored upstream of the guillotine lock. I parked near the pub and walked beneath tall trees down the sloping lawn to the boat. I had been told to arrive at two o'clock but there seemed to have been some rearranging of schedule and it was half-past three before I was required to step on board. I was beginning to get twitchy about being away from home for so long at such a busy time. But as Maurice had said, it was free publicity. As it turned out, the interviewer had not known about my brand-new painting book so I was able to give it a plug. I had actually been invited because 'Lock, Stock & Barrel' was currently being serialised on the radio.

"Good heavens!" I exclaimed when the producer told me, "that's news to me!"

By the time the interview was over and I had driven the thirty-five miles home, it was five o'clock. Maurice did not look too cheerful.

"There's a hotel pair full of Americans tied up on the other side," he grumbled. "They're driving me potty."

"Oh dear. I'll take over now, you have a break."

"It'll be a pleasure to feed the hens," he said, stomping off up the garden.

Across the canal, I could see the hotel boats being filled up with drinking water. It takes them ages. In that situation, the guests come in and out of the shop a dozen times each. As Americans are usually 'doing Europe' (the English waterways featuring minutely in their itinerary), they rarely buy more than a few postcards. I watched an elderly lady with blued hair picking her way across the lock beam and heading my way. In she came and I smiled winningly (I had had an afternoon off!). She spun our drumful of postcards round and round, selecting one or two after much muttering to herself. Then she pounced.

"Aha!" She looked at me accusing, tapping a postcard with a puce talon. "I've been looking all over for this one."

"Really? We do like to have a wide selection." I leant across the counter to glance at the one in her hand. "Oh, that's my own design – you wouldn't find it in any other shop."

"Don't tell *me* that!" She looked positively angry. "It's pinned on the wall of the hotel boat and I've been looking all over for it."

"Oh." I did not know whether I ought to be gratified. She did not make it sound like a compliment. "The postcard is on the cover of my book, too."

She picked up 'Lock, Stock & Barrel' and riffled quickly through it. "Is this on sale in other shops?"

"Yes," I said, wondering what she had against ours.

"I'll buy it later on, then," she grunted, putting it back.

"Fine," I said calmly. "Although you can only get a signed copy here, of course."

"I sure appreciate you telling me that," she said, paying for three postcards. I do believe she meant it.

Maurice heard the tail end of this exchange as he came in with the new-laid eggs. He grinned. The breath of fresh air had obviously restored his good humour.

"The two before spent half an hour poring over the horse brasses," he said. "They examined all twenty-four designs, narrowed it down to two – our own and the Grand Union – then went away with none."

"Too heavy for air travel, I expect. Anyway, it's time to close, thank goodness. They've missed their chance."

We were still fast asleep the next morning when a rat-a-tat on the front door of the cottage startled us out of oblivion. Maurice shot out of bed. I pulled the pillow over my head but I could not deaden the sound of transatlantic voices which were coming from just below the bedroom window. I heard Maurice answer the door and then the slap of his bare feet on the hall tiles as he went through to the shop. Something clinked as he returned. Eventually, the front door thudded, followed by the click of the gate. After a while, Maurice came into the bedroom with a tray of tea.

"Two horse brasses." He put a cup beside me.

"Couldn't they have waited until we open up?" I grumbled sleepily.

"The hotel boats are moving on now," he said placidly. "They were very apologetic."

"Did they tell you to 'have a nice day'?"

"How did you guess?"

Most of July and the whole of August were wet and dreary. We just managed to cope with the grass cutting in the brief dry spells thanks to the purchase of a new hover mower which cropped the part the sheep were not allowed to graze. The latter were a mixed blessing. The ram lambs were very naughty; jumping on and off the henhouse roof which was suffering and leaking in consequence. Lambs love to play king-of-the-castle so Maurice gave them a pile of straw bales but they preferred the henhouse. When we erected the electric fence round the sheep lawn and moved them there, they pushed through it and fell on the roses with gusto.

After a late start, the vegetables had picked up and were doing well in spite of the rain and an army of slugs. French beans and courgettes were giving an impressive yield. I had become disillusioned with raspberries although we love to eat them. I was tired of seeing their suckers popping up all over the place, often six or seven yards away in the middle of the lawn! So I dug a new bed and started to prepare it for strawberries instead.

The sweet peas were amazing; rivalling anything I had seen at Chelsea. I had planted them in a mixture of sheep and chicken manure on the outside of the fruit cage up which they romped, conveniently obscuring the bindweed within. The only problem was that the hearts of the blossoms were filled with miniscule black beetles. There are good beetles and bad beetles. Which were these? After examining the flowers carefully and finding no damage, I concluded that they were harmless beetles. On the other hand, I really grow sweet peas for picking and tiny beetles are a nuisance. Shortly after a vase of sweet peas had been placed in a room, the window would be crawling with the wretched insects. Then I discovered the answer. If the cut flowers were first put in a room with one open window or door and left there for an hour or two, all the little chaps would fly happily away. I believe the infestation is a phenomenon of the east of England because other gardeners of my acquaintance elsewhere have never experienced it.

With Tiffany helping us out again, we were able to spend time giving Warwickshire Lad some much-needed maintenance. One of the penalties of a linear mooring in our case has been the damage done by people on other boats. Apart from the obvious knocks and scrapes along the strake, the most irritating to date was caused by someone fastening the ropes of a big boat to our grab-rail, wrenching it loose from the cabin roof. We did not realise what had happened until water started to lift the interior paintwork and discolour the panelling. It took ages to rectify even after Maurice had replaced the rail.

Occasionally, we took a day off although there was usually a purpose in mind. For instance, we drove to Ledbury to have a look at some new henhouses, having lunch with my sister Cassie and tea with some ex army friends. It was ages since we had had a day out together in summer (if one could truthfully describe that August as summer). I felt sorry for the people on hired boats. August is the peak rate and for most of them it was their annual holiday. We did our best to cheer them up when they came into the shop, and so did Tiffany.

This reminds me of a little story with a less than satisfactory ending.

Back in the spring, an envelope had arrived in the post containing a handwritten note and a photograph of our premises taken from the lock. *Dear Gingers*, ran the note. *How is it? Sorry we passed by when you were still in bed. We enclose a photo we took to prove it.* To be sure, the photograph of the front bathed in morning sunshine showed our bedroom curtains drawn and no sandwich board on the towpath advertising our wares. *We're on our way back down the Grand Union, hope to see you another time. From The Lads.*

"How odd," I murmured to Maurice, crumpling up the note and dropping the photograph into the half-open drawer below the counter.

Ten days later a postcard arrived with a picture of a beach in Cornwall on it although the postmark was somewhere in the home counties.

Dear Gingers. How is it? Hope trade is good and you're both well. From The Lads.

And so it went on. Every couple of weeks we received a postcard, each with a different view and all somewhat dog-eared as if they had been in the back of someone's desk drawer for a number of years.

The postmarks, when they were legible, varied. The handwriting was consistent as if the same lad were responsible for the missives. Gradually, the messages shrank to a mere *Dear Gingers. How is it? From The Lads.*

"How is what?" I asked Maurice when the fifth or sixth card arrived to be added to the growing pile in the drawer.

"Heaven knows," he said, equally intrigued. "I'd like to meet them"

"It looks as if we're going to," I said a couple of weeks later. "This one says that the lads will be coming this way soon and they are looking forward to seeing us."

Every time a group of young men came in, usually to buy beer or lager, we waited expectantly to be told that they were 'The Lads'. Nothing happened. Then, in early September we went away on holiday leaving everything in Tiffany's capable hands. About a week after we got back, a postcard arrived.

Dear Gingers. How is it? Sorry to miss you but your Miss Gregory looked after us very well. Hope you enjoyed your cruise on Warwickshire Lad. From The Lads.

And that was the last we have ever heard. As for Tiffany, she said there had been a number of parties of young people into the shop during our absence but none of them had mentioned 'The Lads' or asked for her full name.

"It's someone with a sense of humour," said Maurice.

"And we'll probably never know," I replied. Unless they read this, of course. In which case we can expect… *Dear Gingers. How is it?…*

= 12 =

LOOK EAST

We set off on holiday on the 3rd of September, a fortnight earlier than the previous year which meant that we were leaving behind a brisk trade. Tiffany enjoyed being busy but we had to make sure that there was enough stock in reserve so that she would not run out of anything before we got back. It required a superhuman effort to get away and I wondered what we had forgotten to do at home. The boat had to be checked over and equipped; clothes and food stowed away. One of our last tasks was to load a new fibre-glass dinghy onto the cabin roof.

Wadenhoe had offered an enticing prospect of the River Nene which I relayed to Maurice. We had been selling licences on behalf of Anglia Water Authority for some years now.

"With an up-to-date knowledge of the river, we would be able to answer most of the questions put to us about it," I argued.

"Irthlingborough was as far as we got," he mused, "years ago. Damned cold, it was. Even Bruce didn't want to go any further." It had been in 1977, when Warwickshire Lad was kept at Copt Heath Wharf.

"This time, our starting point is nearer and we might get further downstream," I said, hoping that we might make it into the Middle Levels, the navigable drains of East Anglia.

"O.K."

It was squally with high winds when we began to lock down Buckby flight at noon with a hired boat from North Kilworth. The crew was competent but the steerer, who was wearing a Walkman and a glazed look, was uncommunicative. I was glad when they nipped ahead of us out of the last lock, letting Maurice close the gates. They disappeared round the bend towards Brockhall woods, leaving us to enjoy the peaceful stretch to Gayton in sunshine.

At Bridge 47, Maurice looked at his watch. "Hm," he said. "Five-thirty. Do we start down the flight or not?"

I cogitated. The Northampton Arm drops down seventeen narrow locks to join the River Nene in the county town. The locks in the Rothersthorpe flight are close together which means either tying up before Bridge 48 on the main line or soldiering on to lock number 13 on the arm. The pound after that is the first one of any length and used to offer a pleasant mooring.

"D'you really want to stop now?" I frowned. "I don't. It shouldn't take us more than two and a half hours at the most."

"It's dark by about eight," he said. "We'll have to get a move on."

We decided to have a go; working like crazy, taking it in turns to run ahead to set the next lock. All the locks were against us and no boats ascended the flight. I must be using up calories (or is it kilojoules?) galore, I thought as I jumped off the boat and sprinted back up a slope to shut the gates behind me. It was half-past seven when we slipped beneath the wooden lift bridge and tied up at a culvert carrying a tributary of the Nene.

"The motorway's not unduly obtrusive," said Maurice, dropping a pair of empty yogurt pots over the mooring spikes. The area had been landscaped into a river walk and he did not want anyone tripping up in the dark.

The fields on the opposite side were newly harvested and dotted with huge, circular straw bales that gleamed golden against the inky clouds and apricot horizon. A heady scent, probably meadowsweet, surrounded us. The next morning I wandered along the towpath, surprised at the number and variety of wild flowers; marsh sowthistle, orange balsam, yellow archangel and hedge woundwort – to name a few. Teazels grew tall on the bank, rising from between the dinner-plate leaves of coltsfoot. I even found a plant classed as 'rare' but probably I made a mistake in identification. It looked like sickle hare's ear but I doubt if it was.

In lock 17, we saw a young man swimming as we approached. He climbed out and immediately dived in again, continuing to do this even as we entered the lock. I closed the gate and Maurice waited for him to get out before he raised the bottom paddle. The fellow ignored him and went on splashing about behind the boat so Maurice shrugged and gave the spindle a few turns. The water dropped a couple of inches, at which point – out he got. Relieved, Maurice shot the paddle up and crossed the gate to deal with the other one. No sooner was that done than –

splash – in the chap went. I fervently hoped he would not be sucked into one of the sluices. He may have been a nut-case but I did not want to be responsible for drowning him. After we had left the lock, I saw a windlass being retrieved from underneath a grubby towel, no doubt to refill his private swimming pool.

Someone told us later that a boy was in the habit of doing this at one of the large Nene locks. In front of a boat's crew, he had dived into the river above the closed top gates as soon as the sluices were opened and reappeared inside the chamber, grinning his head off!

At Rush Mills lock, the engine packed up. I throttled down as the boat nosed in through the gate. The Sabb coughed, sighed and died. Warwickshire Lad drifted among the rubbish in the oily water. I called to Maurice not to open the bottom paddles and threw him a rope.

"Could be worse – I reckon it's water in the fuel," he grumbled. "Condensation, I expect. I'll have to filter it off." It happens sometimes when we have not used the boat for a long while and the fuel tank has been left half empty. There were no other boats in sight so we stayed in the lock while he dealt with the problem. It is the sort of occasion when Maurice wishes that we had a separate engine room giving him freedom of movement. Turning the flywheel over by hand is particularly awkward in such a confined space.

After an hour we were on our way again with, to our relief, a sweetly sounding engine. I was glad to escape the acrid fumes of a perpetually burning bonfire on the lockside.

The Washland flood relief scheme had been created since our previous trip down the Nene. It is one of those rivers, like the Severn, which can change its nature rapidly in times of heavy rain. The level rises, the current increases and the colour alters from clear green to murky brown in a matter of hours. It could be very frightening if one was caught unawares. The Northampton Barrage has done a lot to alleviate this although the river should still be treated with respect. In flood conditions, the water is regulated by the river authority. This entails operating sluices and 'reversing' certain locks so that they are inoperable. Some of the flood control is done automatically; the barrages, for example, are raised after an audible warning is given. This is fine if you do not happen to be navigating the channel between the Abington and Weston barrage gates when you hear the signal. If Warwickshire Lad were midway, our ten horsepower engine would be unlikely to get us the half mile to the other side in time. I have nightmarish visions of being scooped up by the barrage if we made a dash for it! An iron ladder has been thoughtfully provided for the crew of any boat which might be stranded. You tie your boat to the ladder and abandon it; reclaiming it when things are back to normal. Observing the half-submerged rocks at the base of the ladder, I imagine you might find the hull has sprung a plate or two when the water level drops. We made a note to mention this to the river authority.

Surplus water flows through a sluice into two hundred and seventy-one acres of flood plain which support large numbers of water fowl. I grabbed my binoculars excitedly as Maurice gripped the tiller against the cross wind; losing count of swans when I got to thirty.

Weston Favell was the first of the guillotine locks. Another idiosyncrasy of flood control is that locks must be left with the top, pointing, doors closed and the lower, vertical gate raised. This makes for hard work, particularly as the guillotine requires eighty laborious turns on the fixed windlass to lower and raise it.

To begin with, we felt like raw recruits – so long had it been since we worked this type of gear. Over the years there had been changes in the mechanism and the vandal-proof locking devices too. The latter required a special key which we issued along with the licences.

I was anxious to do my share of the work but I did not have the strength required to 'crack' the guillotine – that first mighty effort to start the sheet of metal moving upwards in a full lock. Once Maurice had got it going, I took over at alternate locks and wound it the rest of the way. The water level plummeted with unnerving rapidity.

Alongside Cogenhoe lock was a caravan site and a collection of mobile homes. There was no-one about. We struggled for ages trying to fix the security device in position after we had emptied the chamber.

"There must be a knack," said Maurice when for no obvious reason the locking barrel chose to behave. "I daresay I'll get it eventually."

"We'll be lucky if we get to Peterborough at this rate," I said anxiously. "Coming back we'll have the current against us as well." I could see the top of Whiston lock as soon as we left the chalet village behind. "There's another of the wretched guillotines. My arms are aching, let's stop beforehand."

This was easier said than done. Regulations stated that no vessel should be moored within 100 metres of a lock, sluice or weir except in the course of navigation. But river banks are not like canal towpaths. There is no piling and silt is deposited by the current, preventing even a shallow draught boat from getting near enough for anyone to leap for the bank. We made a few fruitless attempts before arriving at the lock approach. It was seven o'clock, chilly and gloomy.

"It'll have to be here," stated Maurice, pulling in to the side. I jumped off with the mooring rope.

"We'd better haul the boat as far back as we can," I said. "Even then, it's nothing like 100 metres."

"Too bad," said Maurice. "Anyway, we're not obstructing the lock."

The water was rushing noisily along the weir stream quite close to us, hidden by a mass of burdock and nettles. I thought the din would keep me awake but we both fell asleep seconds after I turned out the cabin light and did not stir until the sun was up.

It was a fine day. Refreshed after an undisturbed night and fortified by a cooked breakfast, we set off in good heart and quickly got into a locking routine which made better progress. We were taking approximately twenty minutes per lock.

"The route planner is quicker than we are," I said to Maurice.

"Whoever did the timing probably cruised the reaches at the maximum permitted speed," he said. "I'm sure we're doing nothing like seven miles per hour, even without delays."

We had already decided to stop in Wellingborough to do our weekend shopping. It's a fair distance from the river which meanders through gentle flood plains well away from civilisation. It was half past two by the time we tied up at the municipal quay between the two Wellingborough locks. Friday was market day, we discovered, which made the long walk there and back worthwhile. Three public telephones were vandalised so we abandoned the idea of ringing Tiffany and were back on board by four o'clock.

Ditchford Lock is the only one with a radial lower gate, reminiscent of a particular sort of bread bin. It needed just as much effort to raise the gate but I find it less threatening than the straightforward guillotine – particularly when I am underneath!

a radial lower gate

It seemed a good time to take the dinghy, Puffin, off the roof as there were several low bridges ahead. I had spent many childhood holidays on the Norfolk Broads and with happy memories of rowing myself up little creeks and inlets, I persuaded Maurice to put up with the encumbrance. It was something else to watch out for in the locks, though.

Irthlingborough was memorable to us on two counts, neither of them pleasant. One was a frightful bridge, low-arched and on a bend. The current had swept us through at an angle and we clobbered the corner of the cabin going both ways, try as we would to stay in control. The other was a nauseating stench from a tannery. It smelt more like fur and feathers being converted into fertiliser. These two factors had encouraged us to turn back when we did and were probably the reason why we had not been tempted to cruise the Nene again for so many years.

We were relieved to discover on this occasion that the crucifying bridge had been bypassed by a completely new channel, ugly but placid. The stink, alas, was unchanged and wafted for miles. By the time we were out of sniffing distance, Upper Ringstead lock was in the offing and it was twenty past seven. Maurice managed to get ashore easily and moored the boat legally midway between the weir stream and the lock. Except for the honking of geese and the usual river sounds, all was quiet.

This did not last long after daybreak. To our dismay, nearby gravel pits had woken up. Lorries rattled along a rough track we had not noticed in the dusk, sending clouds of dust in our direction. Maurice's eyes watered and he sneezed.

"Let's push on," he suggested, "and stop later for breakfast."

I nodded without speaking; no point in opening my mouth to be filled with choking particles. In any case, I do not usually say much until I have drunk my first cup of tea. So I put the kettle on and then dressed quickly. Two hours later, we stopped at Denford lock. The chart showed a footpath to the village which boasted a post office and stores. First we had to make our way precariously across the slimy top of the sluices and then through a field. We were immediately surrounded by a herd of inquisitive bullocks. They accompanied us to the far gate through which they were loth to let us pass; standing their ground between it and us, swinging their mucky tails, rolling big brown eyes and licking froth off their soft muzzles. Maurice marched firmly through the middle of the gang with me scampering close behind him. In the village, we found a telephone but no shop although the filling station sold eggs. It was only fresh milk that we were after, but annoying none the less. I always have a reserve of long-life milk and Marvel but they do not taste quite as good, especially in tea.

The beasts had retired to the other end of the field, I was relieved to see, when we recrossed it. After a substantial 'brunch' of weetabix, scrambled eggs on wholemeal toast, ham and some slightly trampled horse mushrooms, we pushed on through the lock. It was noon, overcast and cool.

At Titchmarsh lock, I had one of the most frightening experiences ever while boating. In Nene locks, chains are hung horizontally and fixed to bolts on the inner walls. If a non-swimmer should fall into an empty lock, it would be possible to work one's way along a chain as far as the iron ladder and climb out. When the lock is full, the chains are submerged. We made a practice of looping our mooring ropes round the bollards on the lockside and passing them back to the steerer – in this case, me. As the level dropped, I paid out the ropes. This had to be done quickly as the lock emptied fast. At first, Warwickshire Lad was sucked against the side but as soon as the gate cleared the surface of the water, the boat drifted out. Without the restraining ropes, Maurice could not easily have got back on board.

The first hint I had of danger was when the boat started to tip sideways. I yelled at Maurice who stopped swinging the fixed windlass. He took one look and started to turn it the opposite way to stop the lock emptying. The great gate halted its upward momentum and slowly began to descend. Water continued to escape through the shrinking gap to unite with the river below and Warwickshire Lad was tilting further and further towards the point of no return. I was just wondering whether to abandon ship when, with a deep, grinding noise the boat suddenly fell onto the water with a loud slap and rocked to a level stop. My heart gradually ceased thumping against my ribs and I tried to guess the cause of the near catastrophe.

"Shall I go on?" asked Maurice.

"Yes," I said, "but slowly. We were hooked up on something." Just then I noticed the chains appearing above the water. "I think I know what it was!" There was some black paint off our hull on one of the big protruding bolts. "The rubbing strake was caught on a bolt," I explained. "I'll have to stop holding the boat in to the side and try to keep it away in future." This was not at all easy, we discovered. The suction of the water was very powerful; flattening the rope fenders which we thought might keep the hull clear of the bolts. I sat on the roof and braced my feet against the lock wall but sometimes even that was not enough, Maurice had to add his strength on the shaft.

The next lock was Wadenhoe. We tied up at the jetty where I had been interviewed by Radio Northampton and went for a walk. It was a charming, unspoilt village with stone houses and narrow lanes. There was a general stores which was tight shut. We passed the village hall where the ladies of Wadenhoe had been offering cream teas on the afternoon of my previous visit.

"I could just do with a cream tea now," I said to Maurice wistfully. But the village hall too, was firmly closed.

"Fattening," he said unsympathetically. "Come on – quick march to the top of the hill to see the church and then let's go. We're on to the best part of the river now."

He was right. The Nene wandered quietly in wide sweeps through lush watermeadows filled with grazing cattle, the occasional slender spire of a church through the trees giving away the presence of a village safely nestling above the flood plain.

Alongside a field not far from Cotterstock lock, we tied up for the night; disturbing a vast flock of Canada geese wading and feeding in the shallows. They continued honking their annoyance long after we moored, eventually flying off to join dozens of rooks in a field of stubble. The sun sank in a flame of orange at the edge of some dense trees. Across the watermeadows, the crocketed spire of Oundle church reminded us that tomorrow was Sunday.

We carefully timed our departure the next morning to coincide with a boat coming up the lock. It was the first one we had seen on the move since leaving the main line of the Grand Union. The wind was fresh and the sun glittered in a clear sky. Local boat owners were obviously out for a weekend jaunt. The river was actually quite busy. Everyone waved and called 'hullo'. I got the impression that visitors off the canals were comparatively rare. Spread over the season, we had sold a good many licences but not enough to make the river crowded.

Fotheringhay bridge can be tricky when there is a heavy flow of water. Going downstream you have to keep well over to the left-hand bank in order to get a straight run through the largest of the left-hand arches. The apex is only two and a half metres high in normal summertime conditions. The river was up a few inches but not enough to cause us any problems.

A narrow boat had just entered Warmington lock when we got there at one o'clock.

"Copperkins," I murmured, as it rose level with the lockside and I could see the name. There were four motor tyres hanging as permanent fenders on each side of the boat. Unsightly but effective. "That's the answer," I said to Maurice, "to keep the hull clear of the bolts."

"We'll remember next time," he said.

"And recommend them to customers," I added.

The gear was even stiffer than usual, so we were not sorry to have had our work halved by the other crew. Warwickshire Lad swept beneath the two High Road bridges, one old stone and arched like Fotheringhay, the other modern. The current got swifter as the river broadened, its course doubling back on itself. A light aircraft from Sibson Aerodrome circled overhead.

"Look there!" Maurice pointed upwards as a stick of sky-divers dropped from the plane which continued to circle. The gaily coloured parachutes of the first lot had barely opened before another stick fell, then another and another. I counted as many as fourteen in one drop. They all floated down on the other side of a low hill and disappeared from view.

Wansford station marks one end of the Nene Valley Railway. The steam engine gave a toot as we passed. Sunday must be the day for a train ride on the five miles of track to Orton Mere. Maurice loves steam trains – what a pity we had other things to do.

A delightful group of buildings at Water Newton lock made a perfect subject for a painting. But it was another of those places where it is impossible to get near the bank except close to the lock. One boat was ahead of us, waiting. We came in behind, wondering whether we could manage to drag Warwickshire Lad sufficiently astern to be out of the way while I sketched. Hopefully, I jumped onto the bank. A sailing yacht with mast unshipped zipped round the bend and came alongside. I groaned in annoyance. Without even asking, a man wearing a navy-blue peaked cap tied the boat to our grab rail.

"Hey!" I called. "We've had our rail yanked off once before." The skipper (gold braid on his cap) looked at me pityingly, shrugged and went below. Fuming, I got back on board and undid the rope. He popped his head up and scowled. I glanced at Maurice for support but he shook his head.

"We can't stop here," he said, "and it's too shallow further back. Might as well go through the lock now."

"O.K. I'll make the point, though." I dropped the yacht's warp round our front stud. Navy-blue Cap got quite chatty while we waited – I guess he had only been obeying orders – said they usually went out to sea and hardly ever came upstream from Peterborough. The skipper thought the river was dead boring. As for canals....!

Scores of swallows were swooping above the sycamores on the outskirts of Peterborough, presumably because insects congregate around tall trees. Occasionally, I have seen pillars of tiny black flies hovering on top of our own pear tree on a summer's evening. It was past seven o'clock when we tied up at the Town Quay. I sauntered round the gardens while Maurice fiddled about with ropes and canopy.

" It's a pity we didn't arrive a bit earlier," I said in disappointment. "Chris Barber's on tonight at the Key Theatre – listen." The faint beat of jazz could be heard. We had planned to look at the cathedral and possibly treat ourselves to a meal but there were some youngsters fooling about on a empty cruiser moored next to us. "I'm certain it doesn't belong to them," I told Maurice anxiously. "They don't have a door key and the way they're crawling all over it doesn't look as if they care what damage they're doing."

Maurice came out and glared at them. They sat on the end furthest away from us and sniggered.

"They probably won't vandalise it while we're here," he observed.

"Perhaps we'd better give up the idea of eating in town," I said. "Sunday's not a good day for finding restaurants open anyway." I went inside to see what we had in the fridge. Maurice followed and picked up the guide book to the Middle Levels.

"How long until supper?" he asked after a short while.

"Half an hour – are you very hungry?"

"Not particularly. But the lock-keeper at Stanground requires prior warning by telephone. I'll do that now."

"Fine." I finished what I was doing and poured myself a glass of wine which I took outside. The lads had gone and the quay was deserted except for a couple of fishermen. Two swans accompanying four cygnets cruised by, the large male poking his beak aggressively over the edge of the well in which I was sitting. "Push off!" I said; having gone off swans when I saw one murder a poor little white duck at Braunston. The last rays of the sun slanted on the graceful span of the new bridge carrying the Parkway. Immediately after the bridge, at the confluence of Back River and the Nene, we would turn sharp right into the fens. The very word 'fens' conjured up romantic images in my mind and I experienced a little prickle of excitement at the idea of penetrating these magic waterways by boat.

= 13 =

FENLAND WAVES

On Monday morning we waited impatiently for the shops to open in Peterborough. Nowadays, it is increasingly difficult to find food stores in city centres. All the major supermarkets have transferred to that ecological disaster, the green-field site, and small grocers cannot afford the rent. Under the guidance of a local resident we found milk at a newsagent's and a few other things before returning to the quay. Fishermen were out in force in spite of it being a week day, five of them entrenched in front of the amenity block. Facilities for water, refuse and sewage had been scarce on the River Nene and we had no intention of setting off into the Middle Levels unprepared.

Maurice started the engine and I detached the ropes from the rings set into the quay. He eased Warwickshire Lad forward on tick-over while I walked alongside carrying the slack rope-ends.

"Sorry!" I called apologetically as we approached the fishermen, "you'll have to allow us to use the water point". No-one moved except to scowl more deeply. "The hose won't reach," I explained as I drew near the first man, "unless we're opposite that building. The tap's inside." He muttered an obscenity which I ignored and stayed glued to his wicker basket. I stepped over the rod and fixed the bow rope to a ring. Then I went back and tied the boat on at the stern. Fortunately, our water intake is on the foredeck so I did not have to contend with the other four fellows. I must admit I was a bit scared. There were not many other people about and it would be five against two if they turned aggressive. Warwickshire Lad drifted close to the submerged keep-net although it was not our doing. Maurice blandly uncoiled the hose and unscrewed the filler cap but I noticed that he had his windlass tucked into his belt. With an oath, the man yanked the empty net out of the river and withdrew his rod. His mates stared at us malevolently.

It took longer than usual to fill up with water but by then I had come to the conclusion that it had merely been a battle of wills. Maybe no one had won but at least the tank was reassuringly full by the time we pulled away. Now the other four fishermen gave us the benefit of their vocabulary as the boat passed underneath the huge roach rods and close to the bobbing orange floats. I glanced both ways along the empty quay. Why did they have to park themselves just there, I wondered? Directly opposite the amenity block on the other side of the river stood a factory with a pipe sticking out of its wall. Whatever was being discharged from the pipe must attract fish – or at any rate, fishermen reckon so.

"What a pity the sani-station wasn't built somewhere else," I commented, "it would save a lot of aggravation."

Maurice turned into Back River under the railway bridge. We passed a pub and some moorings and rounded a left-hand bend. In front of us stretched a broad, straight water course barred by a gigantic sluice.

"Is that Stanground?" I asked in trepidation.

"It can't be," he replied. "I must've missed it – back there." Tucked into the shadow of the offside bank was the lock, now receding into the distance. He tried to bring the boat round in a wide sweep but the strong wind was against us and thick weed caused the boat to lose way. "This must be Morton's Leam, it's unnavigable."

After ploughing into the reeds a few times, we made it. I was glad to hear the thunder of the sluice diminishing as we headed towards the lock. It was ten-forty when we came alongside the jetty.

"The lock-keeper asked me to be earlier than eleven so we're still O.K." said Maurice. "Hang on while I see if he's about."

He disappeared up the steps. I stood in the freezing wind hanging on to the ropes. After what seemed an age, he reappeared.

"Any moment," he called encouragingly and vanished again. It was gone eleven by the time I entered the lock, feeling numb with cold and thoroughly neglected. Maurice, up aloft, was putting his weight against the beam and gossiping cheerfully with the lock-keeper. Standing on the counter, I glanced behind when the gates closed. The lower portions consisted mainly of paddles, which were raised. Green river water rushed through the open sluices in a sleek, menacing curve. Spray flew from the churning mass round the rudder which turned this way and that in spite of my restraining hand on the tiller. Puffin bucked fretfully as the current seethed underneath the hull. The lock-keeper signalled to me to move Warwickshire Lad forward as far as possible, which I willingly did. I was even more relieved when he dropped the top paddles and things calmed down a bit. The Middle Levels are used primarily for drainage and he was taking some of the pressure off the Nene, apparently.

As we left the lock, he asked us when we expected to return.

"Friday, probably, if that's alright?" said Maurice.

"Fine," said the lock-keeper. "You needn't phone. I'll spot you from the tractor – we're harvesting just now."

You can see for miles in the fens. This does not apply when you are at water level, though. The flood banks cut off the view entirely. Except for sky. The vast fenland sky makes you feel as if you are on the edge of the world. And how the wind blows!

It took us an hour and a half to get to Whittlesey along King's Dyke, which was straight at first, skirted with tall, rustling reeds. Beneath us, elongated blades of weed swayed in the current. The dyke narrowed and zigzagged into the town. We tied up between high walls and scrambled up the bank to explore. The houses were built of local yellow brick soiled by peat-laden winds. We passed a number of pubs advertising various real ales.

"Let's sample one, at least," said Maurice. "But first, I'd better phone the lock-keeper at Ashline and make arrangements to go through."

We did not need any provisions but noted that there were plenty of small independent shops catering for most needs.

"We ought to stock up here on the way back," I commented as we left the Butter Cross in the market square. Maurice poked his nose into the pubs we passed, eventually deciding that The Boat should have the benefit of our custom. It was right by the water, so we downed a pint each of Elwoods and hopped on board.

At Angle Corner, a great watery crossroads, we turned left onto Twenty Foot River. The names of the dykes referred to their original widths but they are much wider now. This was just as well as it happened. I had reckoned that it was possible to travel a circuit, taking in the town of March, rather than follow the recommended through route from Nene to Ouse. We were, after all, there to explore not get from A to B. I wanted to see as much of the fens as possible. In fact, the Middle Level Commissioners discourage boaters from straying off the direct route. That discovery came later. We had brought several maps and charts which entailed cross-checking. On one of them, I noticed that the headroom beneath a bridge near the far end of the Twenty Foot River was lower than our cabin top. We had passed a lonely fisherman who waved in a friendly fashion so Maurice turned through 180 degrees and we went back to ask him. Yes, he told us, there was a very low bridge ahead. Ah well...

Angle Corner again. There was a chain across Bevills Leam straight ahead so we had to turn left. There is not much room for individuality on the Middle Levels, I can tell you. An hour later we were at Floods Ferry where we turned right for Ramsey. Now we were on the old course of the Nene. It had quite a different feel to it; twisting and turning and clogged with carpets of waterlilies. The banks were low enough for us to see endless fields of potatoes, sugar beet and stubble, which was being burnt with enthusiasm. At one point we were entirely surrounded by black clouds of smoke. Farms were dotted about. They mainly consisted of corrugated roofed barns without homesteads.

It was nearly six o'clock when we reached Saunders Bridge and the junction with High Lode, at the end of which lay the market town of Ramsey. The guide book warned us that boats longer than 25 foot were unable to turn round at the terminus.

"We could stop at the junction, I suppose," said Maurice, "if you really want to see the abbey. It shouldn't be too far to walk."

The entrance to the lode (which has since been cleared of vegetation) was dank and overgrown. Reeds grew tall on either bank, neither of which looked passable on foot.

"Bother!" I said vehemently. "What shall we do?"

"I could try reversing in," said Maurice obligingly, but in a few minutes the propeller seized up and put him off that plan. "What about going on through Lodes End Lock? It's, unmanned." He pointed at the new concrete edifice further up the old course of the Nene.

"No good," I said gloomily, poring over the chart. "We'd never get underneath Exhibition Bridge which isn't far. There's two or three little dead ends but I bet they're just as weedy as High Lode. Let's turn back and go to Ramsey Forty Foot instead."

Half an hour later we had tied up in the Forty Foot Drain just before the bridge. The flood banks were fairly high but steps had been carved out of the peat at intervals.

"Fishermen, probably," observed Maurice, drawing the boat alongside one of them. "How thoughtful."

"We're out of the wind, for once," I said, pleased. "I think I'd like to go for a row in Puffin while it's still sunny."

It was great fun, skimming along the smoky water in and out of the yellow waterlilies and pink arrowhead. I rowed as far as the junction where the wind caught me and sent the flat bottomed dinghy crabwise into the reeds, startling several moorhens. It was harder work going back. I had not realised that there was a strong current running below the surface. The water looked like dark glass. The sun sank and it became suddenly chill; tendrils of mist writhing through the reeds and licking the hull. Darkness fell abruptly and a dog barked.

"It's very creepy," I said to Maurice as I unshipped the oars. "It would make a great setting for a thriller."

"It's been done before," he said. "Ngaio Marsh and Dorothy Sayers, to name but two."

"Those were both set on the Great Ouse," I objected, "and not recently, anyway. I was thinking of the Middle Levels – maybe the Nene as well – maybe something to do with narrow boats."

"Carry on thinking," he said lightly.

It was bright and warm the next day except when a cloud passed across the sun and then the breeze nipped. Ramsey Forty Foot was described as a charming village with attractive 18th Century houses. We never found them. After twenty minutes walking along a B road lined with anonymous post-war dwellings, Maurice looked at the map and decided that we had come to the end of Ramsey Forty Foot. I posted some cards, phoned Tiffany and then we turned back. Almost every householder kept one or more guard dogs. Dobermans and Alsatians predominated, either scrabbling at wire fences or straining at leashes to get at us. We were relieved to get back on board without being torn to bits!

Lunchtime saw us tucked into the reeds next to one of the few fields in which stubble was not being burnt. It was near a bridge called Botany Bay. We lingered lazily, relishing the respite from the punishing guillotine locks, not fussy about how far we got that day.

The river runs through the middle of March. We tied up alongside some old cottages with quaint shop fronts. Tuesday was early closing day and the local museum only opened on Wednesdays and Saturdays, which was a pity. I asked a hairdresser if she could fit me in but she looked at me in astonishment.

Out of curiosity, we continued to Twenty Foot End and turned left. Was the dreaded bridge on Twenty Foot River really too low? Yes, it was. Maurice did a U turn and we chugged back through March. Shortly after passing a boatyard (as deserted at seven as it had been when we called at four, hoping to buy gas), we tied up for the night. A shaggy brown pony was tethered on top of the flood bank. He munched noisily, occasionally blowing his nose. A comforting sound which sent me gently off to sleep.

"Good morning, pony," I said cheerfully, going outside with the Brasso and a rag. The animal raised his head and probably looked at me through a tangled forelock. He snorted and nudged an empty yellow washing-up bowl hopefully. Presumably someone looked after his needs. When the brass was shining, I swept the roof

Good morning, pony

clean of burnt fragments of straw while Maurice saw to the engine. We were away by ten.

"Have you had enough of the Middle Levels?" Maurice asked. "I think I have."

"Mmn." I was reluctant to admit that I was disappointed but that was the case. The drains appear as a grid on the map so one should not be surprised to find that, except for the old course of the Nene, they are straight. This does make for tedium. I had not expected to find so many dykes closed to navigation or such a restricted view from boat level. Even when we could see around us, there was little of interest. The occasional windswept garden of hardy vegetables struggling to stay upright, a row of plastic tunnels sheltering everlasting carnations, acres of rich black peat or sooty straw. The biggest disappointment was the lack of wild fowl. The skies, except for jet planes, were empty.

"Well?"

"Yes," I said at last, "I prefer the Nene. Let's get back on the river. Will it matter if we arrive at Ashline without warning?"

"I doubt it. Let's give it a go."

Floods Ferry, yet again, and a right turn took us into Whittlesey Dyke. At Burnt House Bridge, we paused for brunch. It was then noon. The lock-keeper at Ashline was happy to let us through without delay and promised to phone Stanground and tell the man there our change of plan. We were at Whittlesey by two o'clock; tying up at an awkwardly shelving bank before the sharp bend known as The Briggate. Provisions were low: too long was spent shopping. We returned to the boat heavily laden with wonderful local produce but short on time to get to Stanground before the lock-keeper went off duty.

King's Dyke was as narrow and weedy as I remembered but we had failed to allow for the strength of the current flowing against us. We made a snail's speed past the brickworks, giving us plenty of time to observe the extraction of clay and its movement by a series of rollers and conveyer belts running round the great pit. The stratum of grey clay contrasted with the surface layer of black peat and fell to an unseen depth. Lapwings were grazing a field off which the peat was being stripped. They flew up in a cloud of beating wings as we pushed on.

After that we passed the McCain factory, some three miles distant. I caught a pungent smell. Was it chips frying?

A tractor drawing a baler was being driven around a large field opposite the lock cottage. The lock-keeper saw us and arrived at Stanground almost at the same time as we did. A grey narrow boat was moored at the jetty supposedly reserved for those entering the lock. We clung alongside until the signal was given for us to enter. Water rushed over the top gates in spite of having had no rain for a week, splashing onto the cratch and pouring into the well. When the paddles were raised it was tricky keeping far enough back without crunching poor Puffin.

"What have we here?" observed Maurice as we emerged from Back River into the Nene. A large inflatable dinghy with a powerful outboard engine was whizzing round and round the confluence of the two rivers. The blunt nose of the dinghy pointed skywards. It was not easy to tell whether the dervish behind the curtain of spray had seen us or not. Maurice gave a couple of toots on the horn but he went on circling until, quite suddenly, he shot behind us and continued his frantic convolutions astern.

"Let's go down to the Dog-in-a-Doublet," I suggested. "Then we will have cruised the whole of the non-tidal Nene."

"The navigable part, anyway," corrected Maurice. "We can walk the rest." There is a footpath called The Nene Way which runs from source to sea. It is clearly way-marked. Since then we have rambled along most of it. The upper part, from Badby to Northampton, is especially pleasant.

It did not take long to travel to the sea lock, taking in the 'measured mile' (which has no speed limit), both ways. A visit to the amenity block was vital to our sense of well-being before heading upstream. The same fishermen were ensconced in the identical spot. They did not move as we approached, although Maurice put his thumb on the horn and signalled that we were coming alongside. Suddenly, one of them recognised the boat and hissed at his mates. There was a kerfuffle as they leapt about with rods and keep-nets, dragging everything out of harms way.

"They're learning," said Maurice with satisfaction. I smiled sweetly at the men, to be answered with a vitriolic glare.

"I'm not so sure," I murmured.

We had noticed a sign below Orton Lock on the way down advertising public moorings off the main river. It directed us into a quiet backwater where a brand-new wharf with shiny mooring rings awaited us. The surroundings were in the process of being landscaped. No other boats were there nor was a soul in sight. The evening sun gleamed on the canoeing pool on the other side of a breakwater and warmed the side of our cabin. I removed one layer of outer clothing.

"This is more like it," I said. "Your turn to have a jaunt in Puffin. It will give you an appetite for fresh fen-grown veg. Our days of slacking are over – back to work tomorrow!"

A noisy awakening by an army of JCBs creating the country park around the wharf sent us on our way unwontedly early. Orton Lock was against us although no boat was coming down.

"Odd," said Maurice. "Perhaps I'd better check with the lock-keeper before I empty it." He made the boat fast at the bollards and went off across the great sluices to the small office. He was back in a few minutes.

"It's O.K." he called.

Our boat banged about against the jetty as the guillotine rose and was then awkwardly placed to enter. Anxiously, I sidled into the lock, ending up broadside. With the aid of the long shaft, I eventually got Warwickshire Lad and Puffin organised and roped on. At least the bolts and chains presented no problem.

The day had begun fine but heavy mist drifted along the wooded reaches from Alwalton to Water Newton and Wansford. There was no perceptible current against us in the reaches and the locks were less taxing going upstream. We were able to cruise straight into each chamber; taking it in turns to climb the ladder and lower the guillotine.

An intriguing stone bridge with asymmetrical arches caused us to slow down and seek a mooring at Wansford-in-England (where else?). We tied up at a private jetty at the end of a garden. The old lady to whom it belonged saw us manoeuvring in mid-stream and invited us to use it. She explained crossly that the boat which was kept there had 'gone off without paying'. So we took a stroll around the village, finishing up with a beer in the secluded courtyard of The Haycock. Two businessmen were playing chess with a huge patio set. Maurice watched the game carefully, shaking his head regretfully at one or two ill-considered moves. I waved my purse in the direction of the old lady who was sitting in her bay window as we left, but she shook her head and smiled.

Water was still flowing strongly over the side weir at Wansford although the river level had dropped since our trip downstream. Patches of dried hairy-pondweed on the reed-mace stalks were now two foot above the water instead of eighteen inches. They had been deposited by the floods a fortnight previously when Copperkins, according to its owner, had been stranded on the wrong side of Fotheringhay Bridge. We went up through the lock and closed the top gates. Then Maurice went back to raise the guillotine. He 'cracked' the gate and fixed it with the locking pin. The pressure of the water was so great even after five minutes that when he released the pin he could not keep his grip on the handle. It spun viciously, catching the back of his hand with a sharp blow. I suppose it was fortunate that no worse injury than bruising occurred but he was in considerable pain for the rest of the day.

There are free public moorings downstream of Fotheringhay Bridge but, observing ominous clouds approaching, we prudently passed underneath the low arch and tied up alongside a field. During supper, a shrill whistle sounded nearby. A woman, a small child and a dog were standing on the bank a few feet away.

"This is a private field," she said pleasantly. "You're welcome to stay but it will cost you 50p."

"Righto!" Maurice walked down the gang plank and gave her the money.

"Would you like me to get milk and a newspaper for you tomorrow?" she asked.

"That's very kind of you," I said. "Two pints of milk would be lovely but no newspaper, thanks."

Surprisingly, there was no rain in the night although the next day was deeply overcast. Another boat arrived. On board were some people we knew who asked us on board for coffee. Mike and Liz made films and had once approached Stephanie about some script-writing. We left them cooking bacon and eggs and set off to explore Fotheringhay which is a picturesque village with historical associations. First we walked up the lane towards the entrance to the castle site where Mary Queen of Scots was imprisoned and beheaded. It was hard to imagine its gruesome past as we climbed up the grassy mound covered with thistles and sheep droppings. The windswept summit offered a splendid view of the peaceful river valley.

Continuing up the lane, we turned left to visit the church on the crest of the field sloping down to the river. Honey-coloured pinnacles and airy flying buttresses looked dramatic against the cobalt sky. I thought the interior was spartan and less inspiring. An energetic sprint across the corner of the field beneath majestic chestnut trees took us to the home of our friendly landlady. The little girl was playing in a sand-pit. Quickly, without being asked, she ran inside and came out with two bottles of milk. With a shy smile, they were handed through the slats of the gate and we placed the money in her sandy little palm.

"Careful," warned Maurice as I teetered up the gang plank with the milk. He pulled out the mooring spikes and hoisted the plank onto the roof while I started the engine. It was roughly six miles and two locks to North Bridge, from which we planned to walk into Oundle.

We arrived at a quarter to three. "If we go straight to Anglian Water," said Maurice, "we might catch Fred and Corinne to say hullo." They were the people with whom we liaised about the river licences. We knew Fred Martin well but Corinne Griffin was just a familiar voice on the telephone. Fred had 'gone fishin' so we had a cup of tea and a chat with Corinne and told her our findings up to date.

It was still early so we negotiated two more locks and tied up at dusk alongside Oundle Cruising Club which had a sign welcoming visitors. To be friendly, we went into the clubhouse for a drink before supper and a game of Scrabble.

Rain was in the air as we pulled into Oundle Marina the next morning to buy urgently needed Propane. Ragged clouds outran the breeze. The jetty was cluttered with cruisers for sale. We crept into a slot and tied the bow rope to a post. Maurice jumped off the fore-deck with the empty cylinder and took it to the chandlery. Getting back onto the high bow with a new one needed a mighty effort. I went off with a full bin bag and eventually found a rubbish skip coyly secreted behind the buildings. Then began the task of extricating Warwickshire Lad. Hemmed in by cruisers, there was insufficient room to turn; the wind swept across the marina, pinning us to the wharf. In desperation, I cast off in Puffin and moored the dinghy to a wobbly jetty well clear of the congestion; getting very muddy as I scrambled out into a bog.

Two helpful chaps rolled up and we set about moving several of the cruisers out of the way. Eventually Warwickshire Lad got out and Maurice steered purposefully across the marina towards the exit. I squelched to Puffin and eased my way aboard, nearly tipping myself into the water in the process. Once in control of the oars and rowing strongly across the basin (which seemed suddenly to have expanded),

I began to enjoy myself. When I got to the narrow exit, I could not see whether or not another vessel might be creaming in at the same time. There had been some activity in and out, I recalled. Now, my view was entirely blocked by the promontory which separated the marina from the river. I shouted in vain to Maurice, who had moored Warwickshire Lad by then, to give me the go-ahead. No reply. I chanced it.

We were both relieved to ascend Upper Barnwell lock and forget the morning's hassle.

An arched stone bridge with classical parapet framed the approach to Lilford lock. A pair of swans drifted into a solitary shaft of sunlight. No possibility of a sketch from the middle of the river, I thought, whipping out my camera instead. To my surprise, through the view-finder I spied someone focusing binoculars on ourselves. The person was standing on the lock-side; a car parked on the verge. I clicked the shutter and waited curiously to see who was so interested in us.

"Well, well!" said the observer. "If it isn't the Gingers!"

"Hi!" said I as we cruised into the chamber, looking up at the lady we privately called 'the dragon'. She was actually a water bailiff employed by the river authority to check licences. More than a few sorry boaters had been caught by her and sent to us to buy retrospective permits. Late of the Met, we understood, she was tireless and efficient.

"I hope you've got a permit," she said as she grasped the bow rope, looped it round a bollard and tossed the end back to me.

"Of course," I said smugly, pointing at the galley window, "there it is." She made a note of the number.

"I suppose you issued it to yourselves at half price!" The tone was jocular but her eyes were flinty.

"Certainly not!" I must have sounded shirty because she grinned.

"Can't say I'd blame you." As the water rose, she chatted amiably, telling us that she moved around to different locks in the course of the day. "I keep meeting up with the same boat," she said. "It makes a change to see you. There's not much about. Cheers." She strode across to her car and disappeared up the leafy lane, taking the fine weather with her.

It poured! By six o'clock we had had enough and called a halt below Denford weir. By bedtime, Puffin was half full of water.

"She'll have sunk by morning if this rain goes on," I said to Maurice. "Give me a hand, will you?"

We dragged the dinghy up the sodden bank and turned her upside down. At first light, I heard a lot of banging. A herd of bullocks surrounded Puffin, pushing, shoving and scratching on the upturned hull. The morning was fresh and breezy but fine so I shooed the animals away, slid the little boat back into the water and fastened the tow-rope.

Puffin earned her place in the evening when we tied up below the mill race at Barton. The flow of water divided itself into a myriad tiny streams snaking and tumbling through wiry grass and heather. I rowed laboriously up a channel of peat-dark water where weed dragged like greenish hair until I came to a low brick culvert, a bridge for rabbits. After turning round (although one end of Puffin looks much like the other), I sped back down and spun around as I met the mill-race! This was a thrill worth repeating many times.

It was to be my last adventure in Puffin on that holiday. By late the following afternoon we were on the Northampton Arm. In lock number seven, one of the wooden corners at the stern of the dinghy lodged in a deep crevice between broken bricks. She very nearly sank as the lock filled.

"Onto the roof with Puffin," said Maurice firmly after the last of the lift bridges. I knew he would not want to take her off again until we got home.

And that is where we were, twenty-four hours later.

= 14 =

PLEASE TO REMEMBER

In spite of a fortnight's neglect, the garden was colourful and productive. Sweet peas covered the fruit cage in a tapestry of delicate hues. In front, a second flowering of delphiniums made a backdrop to red and purple michaelmas daisies. There were late roses, fuchsias and scented garden pinks.

I gave a caterpillar-eaten cabbage to a woman who had bought a rabbit on her way through Weedon.

"It's a Silver Fox crossed with a Black Rex," she said. "I couldn't resist it although I've got three more rabbits at home. Have you got a spare cardboard box by any chance? And some newspaper. It's hopping about the cabin at the moment!"

"Sure", I obliged her. "I kept Black Rexes as a child, you know? A pair named Ebb and Flo and a wicked old fellow we called Juicy Joe. He had a horrible habit of peeing straight at you when you walked past. We had to put glass in front of his hutch."

She laughed. "I've heard of rabbits doing that. I'm dreading going home, actually," she confided, "because of what my lodger might have done. The people who feed the rabbits told me there've been wild parties in my house and no end of girls in bed on Sunday!"

Wow, I thought. Maybe rabbits don't have the prerogative!

The tomato crop was excellent and runner beans were still producing enough to eat and sell. The July sowing of spinach beet was just ready to eat. Maurice erected the electric fence round the lawn so that the sheep could nibble it off and save him getting out the mower.

There was still a fair amount of painted ware left so there was no need for me to top up supplies for a while. With luck, not before the end of the season, I hoped. But a single influx of customers put paid to that idea.

Subnormal geriatrics may not be obvious candidates for a waterways holiday but on this occasion, with their minders, they filled two boats. I never cease to admire the patience of those people who look after others who are mentally handicapped. They often have to temper kindness with firmness. The old ladies were allowed into the shop a few at a time; others were told to wait where it was warm in the sun. There was much discussion over gifts. Hand-painted enamel ware was approved by the helpers because it was bright and unbreakable although expensive. They selected the pieces, none of them small, and took the money from their charges who expressed delight and gratitude at the purchase. Feeling guilty of exploitation, I wanted to offer cheaper items but was dissuaded by one of the helpers.

"They've plenty of money," she explained, "and nothing else to spend it on." My feelings were mixed as I wrapped a lovely blue ewer.

Then, when the old ladies had been dealt with and banished from the shop (not by me), the minders returned and bought many bottles of wine for themselves. They asked for carrier bags in which to secrete it. I am not sure from whom! One of them came in a little later to find out the phone numbers of a taxi and the doctor's surgery.

"An old dear's gone and fallen into the boat. Broken her nose, most likely," she said.

Three days of unremitting rain were enough for me to replenish the stock of canal ware. Then there was a slight frost which finished off the outdoor tomatoes and the runner beans. It always makes me depressed when that happens. Winter is in the offing. My order from Chelsea arrived when conditions were perfect for planting. Among other things, I had ordered some ground-cover roses. At the show, they had been trailing down elegant steps but I wanted them to underplant the old-fashioned varieties in 'what I choose to call a rose-garden'. I had not appreciated the viciousness of the thorns. Now they have spread and layered themselves, if I have to remove the occasional weed it is like fighting my way through Sleeping Beauty's bower.

Fred Fielding, who lived in the little toll house at Norton Junction, called in to tell me a droll story. The Pytchley hounds had put up a fox in the field next to his home. The first he knew about it was when his Airedale and a hound were barking at each other across the canal. After the hunt had moved off, the fox jumped out of the shrubbery behind an ornamental trough in Fred's garden and leapt into the canal. It swam to the opposite bank and disappeared across the field in our direction.

"The one that got away," he said, smiling. I wondered how close it was now to our henhouse.

Our property is almost entirely surrounded by a hedge; mainly hawthorn with some ash and elder. It needs more maintenance than it gets but we try to cut it every other year, leaving some trees upstanding to break the monotony of the hedge. It is a daunting task which, doing a few yards every fine day, takes most of the winter. We aim to finish before the birds start nesting. One bright afternoon in late February we were pruning and layering the last stretch alongside the towpath. The sun was behind us, low in the sky.

I heard a scuffling on the other side, followed by a deep-throated growl. It was Bobby, Fred Fielding's old Airedale. Then I saw his master.

"Hullo there, Brigadier," I said, "isn't it a lovely day?"

He looked up (the hedge is situated on top of a bank) and shielded his eyes with a gloved hand. "Oh," he said, "I didn't see you there – I wondered what was up with Bobby." We chatted for a moment or two and then he went on his way. After a while I saw them both returning to the Toll House along the opposite side of the canal. Fred walked slowly and dejectedly; stopping now and then for his arthritic companion to catch him up. I raised my hand in salute but he did not glance my way.

"Fred doesn't look up to much," I said to Maurice.

"No," he agreed. "He looks very old suddenly."

We never saw him again. He died, as lonely as he had lived since the death of his wife, in the tiny, uncomfortable kitchen at the Toll House. What happened to Bobby? A police handler had to take him away before the ambulance men could get near his master. By then, it was too late.

Braunston Tunnel reopened on the 4th April after a closure of five months. It had happened the previous year and was threatened for next. In addition, Crick Tunnel was shut for much longer even than that. Two precious bank holidays came and went with the Leicester Arm closed to traffic, depriving us of many customers. There were also a number of winter maintenance stoppages lingering into the late spring. Living as we do opposite an important lock on the canal system, it has become obvious to us over the years that our customary bad weather between November and March delays and sometimes prevents scheduled work taking place. Also, daylight hours are few. More could be done in one long summer weekend than over several winter months. If plenty of advance warning were given, I do not suppose anyone would be unduly inconvenienced. As it is, there are those who question the cost of a twelve month licence for six months cruising. For ourselves, we only wished that we could cast off from Buckby Wharf and cruise *somewhere* for a week or two in the off season and then come all the way home again. But that is too much to ask while there is apparently no overall maintenance plan and no liaison between sections.

So trade was not as good over Easter as it should have been. The wintry showers did nothing to help matters either. It was very soggy in the garden but I managed to burn the last of the hedge trimmings. Unfortunately, not before one of the lambs got a prickle in its soft little hoof. I had examined the foot several times before I located the vicious thorn about half an inch long. I managed to remove it with a pair of pliers but the poor mite limped for a week afterwards.

Fools Parsley was rampant alongside the driveway which was thickly planted with daffodils. The bulbs looked spectacular but prevented Maurice cutting down the weeds. All the shrubs and trees were showing signs of young leaves. Every morning, a pair of bull finches feasted off the delicate pink flower buds sprinkled over a bronze prunus near the house. Their rosy breasts matched the blossom which diminished daily.

The wild garden became a mass of dog-daisies and the young trees in the spinney were beginning to exert a small presence. I thought I might plant the bank with Kentish Cobs in the autumn. There is an ancient nuttery near Newnham in Northamptonshire. We came across it when we were rambling along the Nene Way. As well as hazel nuts, they grow a catch crop of double snowdrops underneath the bushes. Together, they make a wonderful display in February; catkins swinging above dancing white blooms.

A wet summer followed, with little respite from the wind. The vegetable crop was tolerable except for mangetout peas which must have found the weather too chilly. Then, on 16th October, a hurricane hit the south-east of England. We were woken in the early hours of the morning by the wind roaring in the cypress tree and waves crashing over the top gates of the lock. We were spared the ferocity of the main storm, thank goodness. I will never forget the television pictures of the devastation in Kew Gardens and mighty forest trees laid low along the coast. The length of time it takes a giant oak to grow makes our 'three score years and ten' appear as a blip.

Strong winds persevered throughout the month; making it difficult to work outside. Everything was a battle. You put a plastic bucket on the ground for a second and it flew off, scattering feed or fruit or whatever. The sheep were nervous and uncooperative. Hens went off lay. The outdoor tomatoes were flattened so I made chutney with the Ailsa Craigs. Sweet 100 were too small for anything useful. We kept a bowl of them in the shop and ate them like sweets. The runner bean poles did not fall, thanks to Maurice's architecture, but the leaves were scorched and shrivelled by the wind and small pods failed to mature. Brussels sprout and calabrese plants keeled over. I banked them up and put a tripod of canes round each one but the earth was too soft to keep them upright. When it was not blowing it was pouring.

I was not surprised when the ewes developed footrot. I had reluctantly inoculated them against it but even that and regular footbaths failed to combat the squelching conditions. Sooty's daughter, Frosty, had the viral infection badly in both back feet. On the last day of the regulation dipping period the mobile shepherd arrived with his lorry. I had been up early to put the ewes in the lambing shed before we opened up the shop. It needed two of us to trim their feet. Maurice to up-end the animal and hang on for dear life. Myself to trim the hoof; paring away any smelly rotten portion and slapping on sticky Stockholm tar which had to be pushed well in between the toes. A messy business, as you can imagine, and not designed to make one start the day spruce and clean.

I left them in the lambing shed on fresh dry bedding for the rest of the morning. It is better that sheep are not dipped on a full stomach so I just left them a bucket of water. How they protested! Foghorn bleats, led by Mistake, echoed over the neighbouring fields.

It was lunchtime before the lorry backed up to the field shelter adjoining the lambing shed. It was a huge vehicle, designed by the shepherd himself. Metal sheep-races carried on the sides were quickly unhooked and assembled. One lead up to a small catching pen from which the animals were released into the dip. They actually had to be totally submerged briefly, which they hated. Then they were allowed to scramble out and run down the second ramp to the ground. This was the moment of chaos because they galloped in every direction except back where they came from. I am quite certain that if Maurice and I had been allowed to control the sheep ourselves, we could have contained them within the hurdles placed to guide them into the shed. But the shepherd always had a couple of girl helpers whose last consideration was our property and whose main aim was to pack up and go. They stowed away the metal appendages with frantic haste and deafening noise; terrifying the animals so that they leaped the hurdles and dashed about the garden. They nearly always ended up in the orchard but not before they had trampled over a few flower beds on the way. Being the last day of dipping, the mixture was mucky and the ewes looked a murky green instead of their usual attractive spotted white.

"It'll have washed off in the rain," said Maurice soothingly, "by the time we get back." For the next day we planned to close for the winter and escape immediately on Warwickshire Lad. A bit of a rush, you may think, but the day after that Braunston Tunnel would close for the duration – again.

It was impossible to get away before early afternoon so we failed to make it to our usual spot at Ivy Bridge. Instead, we took advantage of the official moorings at Braunston Turn. The nearby sewage works

Braunston Turn

made itself known occasionally and violently! As daylight faded, thick fog lingered on the water although the sky was clear.

"'Season of mists and mellow fruitfulness'", quoted Maurice as he usually does on that sort of November morning. It was pleasantly mild as we trickled along to Napton Junction with the engine sounding like so many banshees wailing. We tried for ages to get the grease-gun working; both of us ending up thickly coated in same without curing the shrieks. We were actually heading for Calcutt Boats on another matter – a fridge which obstinately refused to light. On our way there, we saw their entire boatyard staff moving four boats to Braunston. "That doesn't bode well," said Maurice.

Vapour swirled across the canal from Napton reservoir, shrouding moored craft and muffling boatyard sounds. We found a slot close to the top lock and Maurice went over to the office. Another boat loomed behind us, its headlight blinking through the fog. At about 5 o'clock, an engineer fixed the fridge which had been suffering from a blocked jet and another chap tightened the engine drive belt. By then, we were enveloped in a real pea-souper. What was more, the headlight had blown in the tunnel and we had not been able to get a replacement bulb.

I could see that Maurice's mood was getting blacker. It was the usual tale of things going wrong with the boat. He cannot stand that. I was sure that it was simply lack of maintenance. Tiffany had gone on to greater things this year and we had not had any free time to work on Warwickshire Lad or even check things over before we left.

"I'm not sure I want to go on keeping the boat," he growled. "It's more trouble than it's worth."

"It's not the boat's fault that it's neglected," I said quietly. "We are submerged in the shop. Sometimes I feel as if I'm drowning in ice-cream and coca-cola. And for what? We're middle-aged now. Soon we'll be too old to go boating."

"It's not just the boat's upkeep," he said. "It's not being able to get any decent winter cruising. There's literally only one route we can take when we leave here and that's to Stone and back the same way. Even then, we've got to leave the boat at Braunston which is darned inconvenient."

"We can still enjoy ourselves," I said, "and we hardly need a headlight for Newbold Tunnel!"

He smiled then. "It's all of 250 yards. You're right. Next year we'll see if we can get another part-time shop assistant to give us some time off."

I riddled the stove and threw a log on the embers. Sparks flew out of the chimney and fell past the window onto the ghostly water. I yearned to be free but that would mean shutting up shop for good. I longed for more time to paint landscapes instead of roses and castles: time to cruise fresh waterways and those we had not seen for ten years: and time to write a novel which might turn out to be a best seller. Hm!

Trouble dogged us up the North Oxford Canal. Maurice replaced the drive belt with one he had bought in Newbold-on-Avon, eliminating at last the anguished noise from the engine compartment. We spent the following night at Stretton Stop.

"Hawkesbury's beginning to feel almost like home," I commented a trifle acidly.

"Now then," said Maurice. "That doesn't sound like you. Anyway, soon everything will be different. It's a long time since we've been on the Trent and Mersey."

"True," I nodded. "I'm looking forward to it."

It was Friday evening when we came within the vicinity of Fradley. We searched in vain, from early dusk until well after dark, to find ourselves a tolerable mooring before arriving at the junction.

"It needs dredging," said Maurice as we tried for the tenth time to get near the side and heard stones scraping the hull a yard out. "The bank's fallen in all along here."

"After the rain there's been, it surely can't be shortage of water," I said.

Finally we made it, at the end of an intermittent line of moored boats opposite the old aerodrome. Maurice removed a shirt from round the propeller in the glare of the security lights opposite.

"We must have picked that up grinding along the bottom," I said. "Let's hope it's not like this when we're off the Coventry Canal."

It was not. As soon as we were up through Middle Lock after Fradley Junction, things improved. I have never understood why the Coventry seems to be the poor relation of all other Midlands canals. Its only flight of locks at Atherstone had one good feature – working side-ponds to reduce the amount of water used. Now, they have been rendered obsolete and Atherstone is notoriously short of water. Why?

The answer I was given was that boaters do not know how to use side-ponds. Teach 'em, then, I'd say!

A short day's cruising took us to Great Haywood; stopping for an hour in Rugeley to do a mammoth shop at the handy supermarket. It was tea-time when we halted at the moorings below Haywood lock. There seemed to be a lot of activity on the pack-horse bridge and at the entrance to Shugborough Hall. We strolled along to see what was going on.

"Bonfire and firework display," said a young man who was setting up a trestle table at the gate.

"Is it open to anyone?" I asked, not having been to a Guy Fawkes party since our children grew up. I am not really in favour of such celebrations. I think they are dangerous, barbaric and a waste of money. However, it was obviously going to be a noisy evening so I might as well bury my scruples and have some fun.

"Sure," he said. "50 pence each. Half-past six."

We live in Guy Fawkes country, so to speak. One of our favourite local inns is at Ashby St. Ledger where the Gunpowder Plot was said to have been hatched. There is a half-timbered building at Dunchurch, on the outskirts of Rugby, where the conspirator himself was supposed to have lodged.

"How about it?" I asked Maurice.

"I don't mind going along," he said. "Wrap up well."

It was a raw moonless evening. The mist had disappeared and the sky was pricked by stars. We donned layers and layers of clothing and were better equipped than many other people. Only my feet froze. Tramping round the spacious park kept the blood circulating to some extent. The classical front of the Hall looked gracious in the floodlights. As the firework display began, I saw a curtain twitch in the private apartments and wondered whether the famous photographer was at work. More likely the Earl's housekeeper, I thought.

It was a good display and well run from the safety aspect. Everyone was kept back behind a rope barrier and Staffordshire folk seemed sensible enough not to break the rules. What I found the most spectacular was the bonfire. It seemed almost to be the height of the Hall itself. We were standing with our backs to the River Trent which runs between the park and the canal. The lifelike Guy on top of the pyramid must have been placed there by crane. When the fire was lit ceremonially, the flames licked the effigy in a thoroughly grisly manner. Once the whole lot was ablaze, the delicious warmth could be felt halfway across the park. My feet stayed numb, though.

Then the inevitable speeches began, at which point we decided that we had had enough. We made a circuit of the rope enclosure, passed the funfare and the hot-dog stands and walked briskly along the gravelled drive. Suddenly, we were in the blackness of dense trees and bushes on the banks of the river and heading for Warwickshire Lad's cosy cabin.

I must have had one ear on the speechifying the previous night, because the next morning I remembered that Staffordshire County Museum had featured prominently. Pearson's Canal Companion was helpful; providing not only information but also a Special Offer.

"Listen," I announced over breakfast, "if we take this with us we should get free admission to one person accompanying a fee paying adult. Good on Michael! Let's visit the County Museum. It's in the old coachhouse and servants' quarters of the Hall."

"O.K." grinned Maurice. "I'll accompany you."

"I'm younger," I said. "You take *me*." The question proved academic as we both had to turn out our pockets to produce enough cash for one when we got there.

The exhibits were cleverly laid out as if they were part of the working heart of a real life country estate. Well-informed museum attendants were dressed in period costume which added to the authenticity. We began with the office of the clerk to the land agent; coat carelessly slung across his chair as if he had just popped out; walls hung with a series of hand-drawn maps of the estate. Photographs of workers looked down on their simple possessions. The childrens galleries showed a reconstructed nursery and schoolroom. Crime and Punishment illustrated the history of law and order in Staffordshire. The Medical Gallery made me cringe, especially the hideous operating table complete with leather straps and buckles. Sports and Rural Pastimes offered light relief. The guns interested Maurice but I liked the garden implements better. Both of us felt at home in a nineteenth century general stores but I would not have wished to live in the rooms of a typical cottage. Around the stable yard we saw the fire service, the smithy, the coachhouse full of elegant horse-drawn vehicles, and the brewhouse. Best of all, with twentieth century people performing tasks the nineteenth century way, were the kitchens. Cook, helped by a kitchen maid, was actually showing a class of real children (in Victorian pinafores) how to make jelly in glowing copper moulds. The butler was polishing silver in his pantry. Laundries smelt of steam and soap, irons were heating and fine cotton garments were airing on overhead racks.

"It was more like time travel than a museum," I said to Maurice as, footsore and hungry, we wandered back across the pack-horse bridge.

"Worth every penny," he agreed, "of one full fee."

The afternoon was spent cruising as far as we could on the Trent and Mersey, as arranged. This took us to the foot of the Stone flight, which was closed. Snappily, we did an about turn and headed straight home. We made it back as far as Burston by nightfall. It was damp and exceedingly chilly. The chimney smoke drifted down, stroking the surface of the water and promising rain.

Sure enough, heavy drops thundered on the roof in the early morning, continuing through breakfast. We clambered into waterproof trousers, cagoules and gum-boots but by the time we had pulled out the mooring spikes it was only drizzling. At Great Haywood junction, when we paused for water *et cetera*, it had stopped. I peeled off constricting outer garments thankfully.

"Shall we have a quick look at Tixall Wide?" suggested Maurice. Deptmore lock, the second one along, was shut so we could not go home that way. But the Wide is rich in bird life and worth a short detour. We saw several kingfishers (or maybe it was the same one playing hide-and-seek), coots, moorhens and mallards galore but nothing particularly unusual. A watery sun glimmered through the trees by the time we negotiated Haywood lock for the second time in two days. I glanced across the park towards Shugborough Hall as we chugged past and wondered whether the laundry maids had finished their mountain of ironing yet!

"Coal fumes are deadly," I choked from within yellowish-black clouds of smoke from our own stove. It was drifting straight into my face. I had taken the tiller at Colwich lock. Now, woodland between the canal and the River Trent was brilliant with autumn colour and in the impressive parkland adjoining Bishton Hall, two dark bay hunters with glossy coats nuzzled each other beneath the flaming foliage of a chestnut tree. "I'd sketch that scene if my eyes weren't streaming so."

"Woodsmoke's less virulent," said Maurice, "but we're out of logs. I'll collect some when we stop this evening. There were plenty lying around on the towpath after Handsacre, I noticed."

"Will we make it that far tonight?"

"Should do," he said, "if we don't hang around at lunchtime."

Roofless Armitage tunnel has been disfigured by the provision of glaring white towpath railings in front of the natural rock face on one side. I stared purposefully at the opposite wall of sandstone topped with gorse in bloom until the concrete bridge swallowed us.

"I want to pull over," I called to Maurice on emerging. There was an inviting wharf alongside The Plum Pudding. It was not so much a drink I was after as somewhere convenient to valet the roof which was filthy with smuts. This meant unloading everything kept on the top; hose, fenders, bicycle, gang plank, shafts, watercans.....

Looking pained, he agreed. "I suppose we'd better have a beer to justify using their wharf", he said.

The canal was on an embankment overlooking the empty pub car-park and the A503. After a pint of Ansells, we mounted the steps to the wharf and set about clearing the roof. Maurice went inside the cabin and left me sloshing about with Flash up top. A large car, horn blaring, swept into the car park with a squeal of tyres and came to an abrupt halt immediately below our boat.

Idiot, I thought, ignoring the occupants. The horn bleeped a couple more times and a man and woman got out and looked up. I took a peek and went on mopping. They did not look like yobbos – more like us when we are respectably dressed. "Hullo there!" called the man.

Then the penny dropped. We knew them. I racked my brains trying to place how and when. They were halfway up the steps before I recalled where we had last seen them. It had been beside the swimming pool of the Panafric Hotel in Nairobi. We had all been on safari together and were just about to go our separate ways to sunny shores.

"Amazing," said Tony. "We never use this road normally." They lived miles away, in fact. "There are road works on our usual route." After meeting us in Kenya, his wife had borrowed 'Lock, Stock and Barrel' from the library. Driving along the A503, she glanced up at Warwickshire Lad and recognised the name. "Di told me to stop when she saw your boat," he added. "Amazing." We all agreed and celebrated suitably.

Nevertheless, it was early when we tied up at Ravenshaw Wood before the top lock at Fradley. Rhododendrons grew along the towpath beneath silver birches. There was so much wood lying around that I suspected someone had been cutting down the undergrowth. I collected a bag of small logs and Maurice got out his chainsaw to cut up the larger branches. It chose that moment to pack up.

"What a nuisance," I said. "With all this fuel lying around for free, too."

"I'll use the handsaw," Maurice said. "This chainsaw has never worked properly since I got it back." He had lent the machine to an acquaintance who ran it dry of oil and ruined it. "I'll have to buy a new one when we get home," he added regretfully. But one of the effects of the hurricane had been to suck the national supply of chainsaws to the south-east of England. There was not one to be had in the Midlands for months.

= 15 =

SHUT THE SHUTTERS

Resolutions, when I make them, are generally the result of a niggling need which has nothing to do with New Year's Day. But as that particular year was superseded by another, Maurice and I found ourselves intent upon coming to some conclusion about the future.

Half the winter had already passed in a frenzy of producing canal ware for the following season. I was beginning to see roses and castles in my dreams. The pungent smell of enamel and turpentine pervaded the house. Maurice's hair was prematurely grey with metal primer and my fingers ingrained with brush-cleaning fluid. Up until Christmas, I had also been teaching narrow boat painting at the Adult Education Centre in Towcester. I enjoyed these weekly evening classes although I disliked driving along the icy A5 in the dark, dodging heavy lorries. I kept hoping that I would be invited to teach in Daventry instead but it never happened.

Painting occupied so much of our time that the garden was not getting the necessary amount of winter attention.

"Let's get an odd-job man cum gardener," Maurice suggested, shelving the main issue, "to ease our load."

"Odd-job *person*," I corrected him.

"We want someone to do hefty work," he argued.

"That's her problem," I said. "We're not allowed to advertise solely for a man."

However, the first applicant was male and started work straightaway. Bert looked fit, said he was retired and accustomed to handling machinery. After being shown around the estate and where the tools were kept, he nodded at Maurice's instructions and then pleased himself what he did. When asked to strim the undergrowth at the base of the hedge and pull out the bindweed, he set off in the right direction but abandoned the task after a yard or two. The next thing I knew, circles of bare earth had appeared around every tree growing in rough grass and he was busy transplanting pansies into them. I rushed outside.

"Bert! Whatever are you doing?"

He smiled. "The way I look at it, the most important thing about a garden is its approach. You want people on the road to admire it."

I looked helplessly at the apologies for flower beds which were still choked with couch grass and buttercup. "But those will have to be weeded now instead of mown," I complained. "We prefer it as it was. I don't care what people in the road think – they're only driving past at eighty miles an hour or on their way to the pub. This garden is for our benefit and we don't want it altered in any way at all. The pansies were in the rose bed because I put them there."

He shrugged and picked up the strimmer. "I don't think much of this machine," was his answer.

"You could use shears or a sickle instead, if you prefer." I said to his departing back.

After another hour, Bert's time was up and off he went after a word with Maurice.

"He's as deaf as a post," reported Maurice.

"Oh! That accounts for it," I said, relieved.

"Hm," said Maurice sceptically. "Maybe."

The next time Bert came, Maurice bellowed orders and I tried to check on progress frequently. He continued in his own way, creating havoc instead of order. I was glad when the rain poured down and we could insist he knocked off early. Notwithstanding the weather, I had to start undoing his efforts without delay. The pansies were moribund because he had merely yanked them out of the soil by hand, tearing off their fibrous roots and leaving a moonscape between the roses. I gleaned turves from unobtrusive corners of the garden to cover the earth circles; hoping the trees had survived the trauma of having their roots exposed. When I discovered that he had hammered a fence post, earmarked for the orchard, clean through the root ball of an uncommon species of young pine, I exploded.

"We can't afford to keep him," I yelled, hopping about in fury. "D'you know what this tree cost?"

"More than a packet of pansy seeds," said Maurice grimly, cutting the strangling twine and drawing out the post like a tooth. Tenderly,

I filled the gaping hole with potting compost, teasing it in among the roots.

He wrote a restrained note to Bert, explaining that we were somewhat set in our ways and would be unlikely to get on with him as our gardener.

That was the last we heard of Bert, thank goodness. No one else turned up from Long Buckby so I went to the Job Centre in Daventry instead. This time, a youth answered the advertisement; clattering up in a clapped-out car with his girl friend. He had perfect hearing, was cheerful and enthusiastic. The only potential snag was that they were inseparable.

"We want one person for two half days," said Maurice. "I'm not paying two."

"That's O.K." said Mick. "So long as you don't mind Lil coming along."

Maurice agreed although I could not see how Lil could do anything but get in the way. In fact, I was wrong. She worked as hard as Mick. I felt embarrassed when it came to pay-day but Maurice refused to budge. I handed out double rations of tea and biscuits, though. Mick and Lil worked fast and energetically, albeit with fingers that were definitely not green. At least they showed no initiative. Most of the jobs they did would have fallen to Maurice so I referred to them as 'Dad's Army'. I dared not let them loose on any of the finer points of gardening. They were unable to tell a weed from a flower and worked at such a tremendous rate that it was hopeless trying to teach them.

My writing had come to a temporary halt; the thriller idea which came to me in the Middle Levels had developed tolerably well in fits and starts during the winter months. By February I realised that more research was needed; research that was only possible by a visit to the fens, not necessarily by boat.

"I think it will mean two day trips in the car," I said, "because I need to check out the Nene and the Ouse."

"Let's make a break of it," said Maurice, "and spend the night somewhere. How about Ely?"

"We can go to the cathedral, too. A wonderful idea."

It is pretty draughty in the fens in winter, I assure you, and the wind is razor sharp. I was not sorry to be in a heated car instead of standing at the tiller of Warwickshire Lad. The different viewpoint means that you can see the network of drains and dykes and get some idea of the enormity of the task it must have been to drain the area.

The morning of Day 1 was spent exploring the mouth of the River Great Ouse and the town of Kings Lynn. The tide was out and beached boats lay stranded above the low water line. Lunch at Downham Market and then on to Ramsey, where I checked up on High Lode and we took a look at the ruins of the Abbey. Another compulsory visit was to Denver Sluice, an awe inspiring structure below which the Ouse is tidal. There, the New and Old Bedford Rivers shoot parallel arrows to the west. Access to both from the Ouse by boat has to be well timed. I noted how awkwardly placed Salter's Lode Lock was in relation to the tidal river. It is manned by a lock-keeper and only navigable for limited periods either side of high water. Boats entering the Middle Levels must pass through Salter's Lode Lock.

"Hm," I murmured to myself. "We'll have to get round that somehow. My villains have to get from the Ouse to the drains without being seen."

Maurice got our boots and anoraks out of the car and off we tramped to have a look around. I found the answer to my problem eventually

"Where next?" asked my long-suffering spouse.

I perused the map. "A place called Three Holes," I said. "It's near Upwell – only about four miles from here – and then we're through for today."

"Discovered anything useful?" asked Maurice as we finally headed for The Lamb in Ely.

"I'll need to rewrite reams," I grumbled, glancing through my notes. "Nowhere has been anything like I imagined it to be in spite of all the reading up I've done. Even a simple thing like a wooden railing has turned out to be concrete.

"Well, that's why we're here," he said equably, "to get your facts correct."

The next morning was drizzly but we spent most of it in Ely Cathedral. Sunshine trembled on the poor headless statues in the Lady Chapel by the time we got there and the rest of the day stayed fine. We walked down through cobbled alleys to the river. Local potatoes showing traces of rich black peat were offered for sale outside someone's back door. I took a bagful and left the money in a plastic dish. Old warehouses crammed with antiques and bric-a-brac delayed lunch at a waterside inn. It was with reluctance that I tore myself away from one of the most intriguing cathedral towns I remember.

"You've still some research to do," reminded Maurice.

"Yes. Sutton Bridge and a look at the Wash."

We parked the car near the dunes on the edge of Godney Marsh and went for another walk. The tide was out again, of course. I could barely see the sea at all. Dodging from tussock to tussock in the direction of France, hair blowing in a wind straight from Siberia, I recalled a story by Paul Gallico called The Snow Goose. My edition was illustrated by Sir Peter Scott, who once lived in a lighthouse visible to the south of where we were.

"Tide's turned," warned Maurice as brackish water began to seep between the mounds of sea grass.

"Peterborough next – a couple of bridges – that's all."

We were home in time to feed the livestock. It had been such a refreshing break that I could not help wishing that we could do it more often. Even Maurice agreed without reservation.

"If your book's a success," he said, "we can research another!"

Winter passed and as the day for reopening the shop crept nearer, my spirits sagged lower.

"I've always looked forward to the start of the season before," I said to Maurice. "How do you feel?"

He was silent for a long moment. "Much the same. It's this problem of winter cruising. When we first came here, we got some splendid holidays in November, so I didn't mind watching other boaters having a good time in the summer. But lately, it's been virtually impossible to go anywhere except up the Coventry Canal."

"The shop premises would make a splendid living room," I said wistfully. "Perfect for use as an artist's studio with the large north-facing bay window, too." I got into my stride then. "We could leave some of the shelves for books and move the stove into the hearth. The original fireplace is behind all that haberdashery."

"Yes. You can write and paint and I'll become a publisher and picture framer." He grinned. "It'll only be my fifth career to date!"

"Are you serious?"

"I don't see why not."

"When?"

"At the end of the season. Let's make this our last."

"O.K. It's time for a change. We've been here for ten years as shopkeepers, it'll be fun to try life at Buckby Wharf as private people."

"We can do a bit more boating, too," said Maurice, "all the year round."

a bit more boating

"Ah!" I said. "What about the sheep? They can't be left unattended."

"We'll have to sell them," said Maurice. We both looked glum. One should not get fond of farm animals but we were.

"Sooty and Mistake aren't young," I said. "If they lamb successfully this spring we can sell them as 'ewes with lambs at foot'. They'll fetch a good price if each has at least one ewe lamb."

"If..." said Maurice. "Perhaps we'd better keep Frosty and Patch for the summer to keep the grass down and sell them in the autumn. After that, it'll just have to grow long."

"We'll see about them when the time comes," I said. "The first challenge will be this year's lambing."

I need not have worried – it went off more smoothly than in many other years. Mistake lambed first, in front of the kitchen window on the sheep lawn. She complained loudly but there were no problems and although the weather was fine, it was reassuring to put the little family in the lambing shed overnight. She had two healthy ewe lambs. Sooty waited a fortnight as usual; lambing with no fuss early in the morning. By then, the shed was free and the older lambs were gambolling about merrily. Jacob lambs are friskier than hybrids and very playful. She had one ewe and one beautiful ram which I decided not to castrate.

"He'd make a first-rate tup," I said to Maurice, "so I'll leave him entire and give him a chance to escape the butcher."

All six were sold to the same lady within hours of the advertisement appearing and several potential buyers were disappointed. We see Sooty and Mistake occasionally when we pass through Staverton. Even though they are part of a bigger flock we can pick them out easily and it is interesting that they still keep close to each other. A farmer who owned a flock of long legged Soay sheep, another primitive breed, said that he would be happy to buy our remaining two ewes, if and when we decided to sell them.

July that year was reputed to be the wettest since 1936. Boaters were predictably disgruntled. Knowing that this was our last year's trading made us more patient than we otherwise might have been. The grass grew lush; Frosty and Patch being unable to keep pace with it. One evening, I walked up the orchard close behind a small rabbit. It was not really scared of me, just preferred to be in front. My efforts at chicken-proofing the hedge were almost a match for it until we arrived at the oak tree in the top corner where it vanished. I turned to find that the young ewes had been playing 'grandmother's footsteps' behind me! In the same moment, I spied a spread of mushrooms, the first glut for several years.

Another evening, we heard the piercing sound of a burglar alarm which Maurice discovered was issuing from a narrow boat tied up near ours.

"It stopped when I stood on the stern," he said, "then started again a minute later."

"Perhaps it's a gas-alarm?"

"There's no smell of gas. The police have been told, anyway."

After a short time, the police arrived, closely followed by a fire engine and team. The boat was bow-hauled alongside the water-point where the fire appliance could reach it. After testing for gas, the firemen easily gained access through the stern doors. Although there was a large padlock on them, the doors had externally screwed hinges. In the men went, turned off the alarm, left a calling card, came out and screwed the doors on again!

We had a surprise visit in August. For some thirty years our shop and cottage had been owned by a lady well known to working boat families. Her name was Mrs Griffiths, and she had been left the property in trust by old Mr Lovelock who built the place in the early twenties. I knew when we moved in that Mrs Griffiths, now a widow, lived in sheltered accommodation in Long Buckby but we had never met her. I certainly would not have recognised her daughter. But Debbie, our new assistant, did.

"I'm sure that's Mrs Griffiths' daughter out there," she said to me. "She's just been in to buy an ice-cream."

I looked through the window at a couple sitting on the lock beam. A thought struck me and I went outside.

"Excuse me," I said bluntly, "are you Mrs Griffiths' daughter?"

"Yes," said the woman.

"Would you like to come in and have a look around?"

Her face lit up, and that of her husband as they quickly accepted. They had already seen inside the shop which was virtually unchanged except for new windows. She admired the parlour with its pretty Laura Ashley wallpaper and curtains; telling me that it had never been used for anything other than storage.

"And billiards at Christmas", added her husband.

I was told how the boat women used to come in with a huge order to be filled in the time it took the lock to do the same. I recalled the tunnel-opening and the rally and thought that the only thing that had changed were the human values.

We trooped upstairs. "It all looks so lovely and cared for," she said. "I always knew it could be like this some day in the right hands."

I was pleased and yet I felt guilty because we had decided to shut up the shop shutters for good. I won't tell her, I thought, and spoil her memories.

"Did you ever know Matilda?" I asked, thinking of the young woman who painted the Buckby cans which old Lovelock passed off as his own as far back as the thirties.

"Aunt Mattie – yes. She had a sad life, you know? Killed herself, in the end."

"So I heard," I said. "How did she do it?" I had always dreaded learning that she might have hanged herself from one of the hooks in the shop ceiling.

"Drank Lysol, she did."

I shuddered. "Would you like to have a look outside?"

"Aunt Mattie planted the oak tree," I was told on a lighter note, "from an acorn. She was only a child, Mum said, and pleased as Punch when it grew."

"Really? I'm so glad you told me that. It must be about eighty years old, then. I've often wondered."

Both of them enthused about the garden, not least over the soft fruit and vegetables.

"Potatoes, that's all we had," she said.

"Often tried to get your old man to keep sheep," said her husband, looking at ours. "But he wouldn't. Had a pig, in the war."

"I used to sit in the sun there," she said, looking at our garden furniture on the terrace. "Not that we had any deckchairs or tubs of flowers or anything. But it's a real sun-trap." She gazed around as if she was imprinting the whole scene on her mind. "We won't be coming back to Buckby again," she said. "Mum died two weeks back."

"Oh!" I said. "I'm so sorry."

"We've been to choose the headstone, that's all. Then I wanted to come down here and have a look at the old place...... thanks ever so for taking us inside and that...."

"I'm glad that Debbie pointed you out to me," I said, "so that you could see it is well loved."

"It's obviously that," said her husband. "Goodbye."

= 16 =

SKETCHING SUBJECTS

The winter stoppage list, when we got hold of it, told the same old dreary tale. I was even more convinced that shutting the shop was a good decision. We could have repeated our Coventry trip or gone north on the Grand Union as far as Kingswood Junction and no further. Hatton 21 twice on consecutive days did not appeal to us, and with the prospect of unlimited cruising the following year, what was the point?

Thus we spent a mild winter absorbing the business premises into the domestic quarters and thoroughly enjoying ourselves in the process. Structurally, we did very little other than removing the wooden counter which turned out only to be fit for firewood. Having been installed when the shop was built, it parted company reluctantly. So did the partition between the customer area and what had originally been Lovelock's office. When all that was taken away, we were left with an oak post from floor to ceiling.

"We could make a feature of it, I suppose," I said doubtfully. "But it's in rather an awkward place."

"If it's not weight-bearing," Maurice said, "I'll have it out." He shook the post which did not budge so he squeezed himself through the trap-door into the roof to examine the problem from above. It yielded no definitive answer and we spent a couple of days agonising and discussing it with friends before he bravely cut the post out. The ceiling did not fall down so he eased out the stumps which were fixed with five-inch angled nails. We tidied up the tongued and grooved boards on the ceiling and took out all the hooks except the large iron ones designed to carry Buckby Cans in the old days. I felt that these were part of the history of the building and should be left. The rust was removed and then they were painted glossy black. The watercans from Warwickshire Lad are stored there when we are not cruising and bunches of herbs and dried flowers hang there all the year round. After that it was just a question of wall-covering, carpet, cheerful curtains for the wide windows and a thick velvet one to screen the shop door. The result is now the most useful and comfortable room in the house.

There is almost as much red tape in winding up a business as starting one, we discovered. Not that trade was ceasing entirely - it was to be conducted in a different way. Or so we thought. The Inland Revenue had other ideas. The mere suggestion that I should substitute Studio for Stores in the business name generated a stream of correspondence and an inspector was sent round to make sure that we really had closed the shop. In her turn, she satisfied the District Council that we should not be liable for the Uniform Business Rate, for which we were grateful. Extricating ourselves from V.A.T. was easy.

Deryn, the lock-keeper's wife, was happy to look after the hens when we were away, so they were reprieved by us (if not the fox). Lucifer was to become an anxious boating cat.

In early April, Maurice tries to attend the annual dinner of his old regiment. It usually takes place in Warwick.

"How about going by canal this year?" he suggested, poised to accept the invitation. "If I haven't got to drive home, I could drink my quota of port for a change."

"Perfect," I agreed. "It will initiate Lucifer and give us the chance to check that everything's working properly on the boat before we go on a longer voyage."

The poor cat was terrified when I first took him on board. If he had been boating as a kitten, he may not have been so frightened. I shut him in the cabin for a while before the engine was started but he yowled non-stop. As soon as we set off, he hid under the bed and did not emerge until Braunston Turn. The sun was shining and I sat in the well as we cruised towards Napton. After a bit, he reluctantly joined me. Everything was fine until we went under a bridge which he obviously thought was attacking him. Whoosh! He vanished. We stopped at Wolfhampcote to give him a comfort stop, having taken the precaution of providing him with a collar and lead but the alien environment petrified him even more, so I lifted him in board and tipped cat litter into a tray. He came into his own at night when the boat was quiet and still; prowling, purring, munching Go-Cat noisily and scuffling Fullers Earth all over the newspaper spread on the floor. At dawn, he curled up heavily on my legs.

On arrival in Warwick on Saturday afternoon, we chugged slowly past Nelson Wharf where Kate Boats were busy turning round their fleet and came to a halt on the other side of the bridge. From there, it was barely a ten minute brisk walk for Maurice up to Westgate to meet the rest of 'the old and bold'.

After he had marched off in his finery, I sat outside sipping a glass of wine and waiting for the sun to set on the muddied water. A flock of mallards swam past, shattering the mirror-like surface and breaking into my reverie. I had been considering that reflective colours are almost identical to the original but overlaid with a clay-brown wash. Not easy to capture in paint, I thought. In any case, I had forgotten to bring any. I resolved never to stir away from home without my sketching things in future. Daventry Public Library had recently opened a new exhibition room which we had rashly booked for the month of March. There were roughly eleven months before my first one-man show. After taking measurements of the space involved I reckoned that at least forty pictures would be needed to fill the walls. It was to be a considerable challenge for both of us, as Maurice would be doing the framing.

We had paid a visit to the Spring Fair at the National Exhibition Centre in February, not for gifts as had been our habit in the past, but for picture framer's equipment. We now had mitre cutters, cramps, mat cutters, mountboard and lengths of moulding in various profiles and different wood grains. But first, we needed the art-work. The theme of my show was to be 'Canal and Countryside', so in planning our cruises we had to take account of possible subjects to paint.

I have always preferred to work from the life. For instance, we hastily moor the boat when I spy a suitable subject and stay there until I have practically completed a picture. I might put the odd finishing touch to it before framing. Then, quite possibly, it is sold and I never see it again. Even if I were able to return to the same spot, circumstances will have changed and the view may not be in the least 'paintable'. Old buildings get knocked down, ugly new ones erected, vegetation cleared, bridges and locks rebuilt. Maybe the light is simply wrong. Maurice usually takes a photograph of the subject when I begin a picture but only occasionally do the two bear much resemblance to each other. The camera never lies, it is said. Maybe – if accuracy of perspective and the relationship between buildings and other man-made structures are all you want. But when it comes to interpretation and colour, the combination of the human eye and a palette give a broader and more subtle spectrum, particularly in the tender light of spring and autumn. The camera can be be a useful tool to the artist but not a substitute for reality.

I only have a handful of those forty paintings left in my possession which is sad. Now, I try to sketch rapidly, capturing the colour and the feel of a subject. Later, perhaps with the help of a photograph, I will develop it into a separate, saleable picture in the studio. The sketches I keep.

School terms no longer dictate our holidays, so we tend to avoid those times of year when the waterways are busy and queues form at lock flights. The gardening calendar influences us instead; sowing and planting have to be carefully planned – not to mention harvesting!

May is a good month for cruising if the two bank holiday periods are avoided. Spring has usually arrived: hawthorn blossom scents the air and shelters the towpaths from cool winds. We set off from home on the 4th, heading for the South Oxford and planning to dawdle. It was blissfully hot as we mounted the Napton flight where, for some reason, a couple of the pounds were gratingly dry.

I remember an occasion when there was an emergency stoppage at the lock by Shut Bridge. We were instructed to halt in the lock above for several hours. I sat on the beam and painted the golden autumn scene in front; sheep grazing the hill on which the windmill stood guard, colourful boat stranded in the half-drained pound below, which was flanked by russet hedges dotted with rose-hips. Meanwhile, Maurice solved chess problems in the sunshine. After a time, another boat arrived behind us. Engrossed, neither of us paid much attention. Suddenly, the air sizzled with abuse from the irate crew who assumed that we had chosen to block the navigation for no other reason than for me to paint a picture!

Fenny Compton tunnel came as a nasty shock. Where was the wooded cutting of the past, alive with birds and small mammals? Landscaped – which meant that all the trees and bushes which had colonised it since the lid was taken off the tunnel in 1868 had been torn out and burnt. No self-respecting rabbit or fox would inhabit it now. I doubt whether there is a bluebell, blackberry, or dog-rose left. Suburban-type saplings had been planted in the raw earth which had terraces bordered with small stones. The angled slabs of granite which edged the whole of the Oxford Canal at one time had disappeared. The bank now sloped up to the terraces. We motored gently along, dismayed to see the lapping water shifting the loose earth into the canal. It was easy to imagine the result if a canal-cowboy creamed past. Water-plants had been inserted through slits in plastic sheets which were weighted down with loose rocks. Many of these had already become dislodged and torn fragments of plastic floated in the channel. A chewed-up mass caught on a tree indicated someone's displeasure at having it round his propeller!

Earth moving of some magnitude was also going on at Claydon which I remembered being face-lifted into a canal-side walk not many years before. The towpath and lock surrounds were piled with inhospitable granite chippings and seesawing planks offered the only access to the lock gear.

"I wonder if all this is connected with the building of the M40," suggested Maurice.

"Maybe," I said. "I suppose we'll discover one day if we ever drive along it." I always knew it would not do anything to improve the Oxford Canal – we had been pleased when the project was shelved.

Cropredy was unaffected, luckily. I already knew exactly the position from which the best view of the bridge and lock was to be had.

"Bother!" I grumbled. "There's another boat there." We found a space some distance further on and I walked back to see whether I could work from the towpath. "No good," I reported to Maurice, "the boat obscures the view. It looks like a permanent mooring, too." We moved on round the corner to get away from the powerful pong of pigs opposite and tied up. Determined not to be thwarted, I found a subject straight away. Hopping over the fence to look at the river Cherwell, I discovered a splendid misshapen old willow overhanging the stream, the evening sun glinting on the silvery leaf buds. I made a quick sketch of doubtful merit. But with the sun in a different quarter the following morning, a broken hurdle, a bent willow and a mellow barn made a pleasing cameo.

Water is in itself an inspiration and a challenge. It can be glassy, gently rippled, or rough – sometimes simultaneously in one stretch of waterway. It is always full of colour. Creating the different effects with paint requires a variety of techniques, some of which come off and others that fail. I constantly study the paintings of artists such as

Monet and Turner to see how they did it. This can lead to a profound sense of inadequacy which might cause me to give up trying if I were not so stubborn by nature.

Between Cropredy and Banbury, we came to the first of the motorway works proper, which crossed the canal three times in all. The weather had been dry for some time and dust created by the vehicles was appalling. Between Haddon's Lift Bridge and Grants Lock, work was progressing in earnest. Lorries of spoil took it in turns to hurtle over the temporary bridge across the canal, smothering the waterway in a lingering yellow fog. We hung back, timing the lorries, wondering whether the interval was sufficient for us to escape unchoked. We just made it at full throttle.

The towpath crosses Aynho Weir gracefully where the clear water of the River Cherwell intercepts the murky depths of the Oxford Canal. Immediately to the south of it, a bridge of local stone stands close to the top gate of Aynho Weir Lock. Although the level only drops a foot, the diamond shape of the chamber enables sufficient water (provided by the Cherwell) to fill Somerton Deep Lock at the end of the next pound. I found the unusual shape of Aynho made it an awkward lock to negotiate without scraping our paintwork on the harsh coping stones. Almost as soon as we were through, we tied up in the late afternoon sunshine. I was undecided which of the attractive stone structures to paint, eventually choosing the lock with a glimpse of the weir visible through the arch of the bridge. Next time, I will have a go from above the weir perhaps – or maybe repeat myself? I no longer own the picture I did that day and it was one of my favourites.

We stopped early the following afternoon for several reasons. The Intercity line comes and goes throughout the length of the Southern Oxford Canal, sometimes too close for a decent night's sleep. We have become attuned to the places where the two are separated by a tolerable distance. A comfortable depth of water is another criterion. I was also keyed up to sketch and on the look-out for a subject. When the ideal spot presented itself on the non-towpath side, we hove to. Tall trees dressed in delicate spring splendour clothed both banks and were mirrored in the glassy water. Honeysuckle and travellers joy touched the surface where young green shoots pushed their way up between last year's bleached reed-mace stalks. Beyond the towpath, the River Cherwell gurgled its way to Oxford.

Delightedly, I placed my easel and stool on the bank, confident I was not obstructing a soul, for there were none about. I was about two thirds of the way through when I observed that the water in the canal was no longer motionless. It was sliding in the same direction as the river.

"Someone's coming up Pigeon's Lock," I said to Maurice. "I hope they don't moor right beside us."

"I bet they do," he murmured, nose in book. A few minutes later a narrow boat rounded the bend in front. A man standing on the foredeck saw Warwickshire Lad alongside the old quarry wharf and yelled back to the steerer. He threw the tiller over and headed straight for us. I put down my brush and stared in dismay. The picture had been coming on so well – one of my best. Maurice looked at me sympathetically. "Could you finish it in the morning?"

I was too upset to reply. He knew as well as I did that even if it were fine, the sun would be on the opposite side. The boat crunched against the stone piling in front of ours and the man jumped off with the rope and started to hammer in the spikes. I almost packed up then, but I wanted to finish the picture so much that I went on sitting there.

The man jumped on board and went inside. Someone else erected the T.V. aerial. Ripples subsided and again reflections glimmered. My ill temper evaporated. Think positive, I admonished myself. Put the boat in the painting; it's not bad-looking and you haven't done the water yet. I worked hard until the light began to fail and dim the colours. Maurice helped me stow my gear as a second boat turned up and stopped close behind us. This one disgorged children and dogs but by then it did not matter.

The River Cherwell flows into the canal below Baker's Lock. We sped with the current past Busby's Spinney where osiers stood with their feet in the shallows until we came to Shipton Weir Lock. This is another diamond-shaped chamber designed to accommodate surplus water when the Cherwell is in spate. The river leaves the canal above the lock; the short weir stream making an idyllic mooring. I surveyed the scene with narrowed eyes.

"No..o," I said at last, "the composition isn't quite right." I turned round to find Warwickshire Lad disappearing into the lock without me, so I guessed that Maurice had no intention of giving me the opportunity to dally.

Two more locks were all we managed to do before we were forced to stop where there was nothing worth sketching – not even a duck! We were almost in Oxford, too, where we had hoped to buy supplies. As we approached one of the Southern Oxford's distinctive lift bridges, of which only a few remain, we saw a boat coming the other way. It was not clear which of us was the nearer, so we both pulled into the side and dropped a crew member. In that moment a JCB rumbled out of a farmyard on the right and headed for the bridge. Maurice and the chap from the other boat paused on either side of the JCB which was blocking their access to the bridge's mechanism. I hung on to our ropes expecting the machine to shift out of the way any second to let the two boats through. Not a bit of it! The operator, assisted by two more men wearing protective headgear, industrial gloves, shorts and trainers, proceeded to pick up a collection of railway sleepers lying on the bank and place them on the bridge. Sleeper number one was wrapped in chains which were hooked onto the JCB and the men retired to a safe distance while the sleeper was danced into position, spanning the canal. By the time sleeper number three was in the air, I was bored with holding ropes, so I tied the boat up temporarily and approached the danger zone warily.

"What's going on?" I asked Maurice, who dragged himself away from gossiping with the crew off the other boat.

"They're strengthening the bridge to take the JCB across," he said.

"They might have let both boats through first," I argued reasonably. "Anyway – what for? There's nothing over there except an empty field."

He shrugged. "Dunno. They're not very communicative." We both watched the antics of the contractors in silence for a while. A foreman turned up and a discussion was holding up progress.

"They'd have finished by now if they had shifted the planks by hand – two men at each end," I said.

At last the foreman pronounced the bridge suitably strengthened and the JCB crossed the canal, not without getting stuck once or twice in the counter-weight mechanism. We scarcely dared breathe in case they smashed up the whole edifice and blocked the navigation. Then they went through the laborious reverse process of removing the railway sleepers and stacking them on the far bank.

the JCB crossed the canal

The operation had occupied the entire afternoon. The crew of the other boat, which had just left its hire base, were not too pleased at forfeiting hours of cruising so unnecessarily.

"The shops will be shut by now," said Maurice, "so where shall we aim for?" We had told Bruce and Becky of our imminent arrival but not exactly when to expect us.

"Isis Lock? If we can find a space."

"Doubt it," said Maurice, "but we'll give it a go."

At one time, it was easy to moor between the lock and the canal terminus opposite Worcester College. But now all the moorings are residential ones of dubious legitimacy. It does nothing to encourage canal boaters to explore Oxford. Perhaps the town gets more than enough tourists without us?

As I jumped off the bow onto the spit of land in front of the iron turnover bridge above Isis Lock, Maurice announced his intention of turning Warwickshire Lad round and reversing into the dead end. By the time he had winded, I had run down the towpath to the terminus and back.

"Nothing doing," I puffed. "The only space is right at the end which is choked with refuse. The dustbins don't look as if they're ever emptied either. It's revolting there."

"Oxford turns its back on the canal," said Maurice. "I saw a space opposite the boatyard – we'll try that."

We cruised slowly back. A concrete pill-box near the bridge had been taken over by three of Oxford's homeless people. They had built a fire on the towpath and lounged round it; unlabelled bottles to their mouths. We stopped short of a bridge just past Orchard Cruisers. Not caring to leave the boat unattended, Maurice went off to telephone while I fed Lucifer.

"Bruce is away tonight," he said when he got back, "but Bex will come to supper on her own."

It was not late when Becky left. Maurice walked with her to the car park.

"The meths drinkers are stoned out of their minds now," he reported. "Another one has joined them, plus dog."

"What a life," I said, listening to the slurred voices rising and falling.

They were still there in the morning, wrapped in blankets close to the embers of the dying fire. The man with the dog could not have been more than thirty. The others looked old, canny and watchful.

We reckoned that Warwickshire Lad would be safe enough in full view of the boatyard which was humming with activity by now, so locked up and set off with shopping bags. Criss-crossing the residential grid called Jericho we came to Walton Street which is on a bus route.

"What luck!" I said, when I saw the stop. A bus arrived within a few minutes and we hopped on.

"Wrong way!" said the driver. Everybody sniggered. Off we got and waited at the stop on the other side of the road until a bus could take us into town. We went to the indoor market and loaded up with groceries; even buying some coley as a treat for Lucifer. Then we browsed in bookshops. Walking back past the Ashmolean, I saw that an exhibition of paintings by the family of Pissaro was on, so in we went. Not very impressed by Camille's relations, we were just leaving when Maurice noticed a subsidiary exhibition of Turner's lesser known works. That *was* exciting.

With smoke curling from the chimney and a cabin light left on, we hoped the boat looked occupied when we went out for the evening. Bruce and Becky arrived in pouring rain to collect us in the car and off we went.

Cotton-wool clouds scudded across a sky of washed blue by mid-morning the following day. Puddles lay on the bridge, disintegrating paper litter and dissolving canine excrement. I picked my way towards a corner store for fresh milk and was side-tracked by a shop selling Ghanaian goods. I bought a gaudy mammy-cloth waist-coat to remind me of army days in Accra and rejoined Maurice and Lucifer on board Warwickshire Lad.

"This is only the second time we have stayed for two nights at one mooring," he said as he knocked out the spikes. "D'you remember the last?"

"Llangollen in 1976, the year of the drought. We'll have time to go north again now – and often stay two nights in one place – there's no hurry, anymore."

= 17 =

SHAKESPEARE OR BUST

The Queen's Silver Jubilee had been the occasion of our last trip down the southern section of the Stratford upon Avon Canal. I remember how the Union Jack we fixed to the headlamp dripped forlornly in the drizzly rain which persisted throughout the public holiday. The National Trust operated the canal in those days and the condition of the locks had deteriorated since the reopening of the waterway thirteen years before. As the situation worsened, the levy increased. We felt disinclined to repeat the agony. Now that British Waterways was in charge, however, things were reported to have improved.

We planned to complete a circuit popularly known as The Avon Ring. At Lapworth, in Warwickshire, a short branch links the Grand Union with the Stratford upon Avon Canal at Kingswood Junction. Here, it is possible to cut into the 'ring' and begin the circuit where the two Stratford sections meet. The northern section had never declined quite to the same extent as the southern which was nearly closed altogether in 1955. It was entirely thanks to vociferous campaigners that the canal was officially reprieved in 1959, by which time it was unnavigable except by canoe. Those same campaigners persuaded the National Trust to acquire the waterway with a view to restoration but it was to be another five years before it was reopened by Her Majesty The Queen Mother.

It was mid-July when we left home, hoping to be back in early August. The weather was none too bright as we headed north up the Grand Union for Kingswood Junction. Cloud cover melted away as we entered lock 21 by the old National Trust office. In the late sixties and seventies, the first couple of pounds were known locally as 'hippie-land' and occupied by residential boats. There was a story that when the delightful television film, 'Shakespeare or Bust!' was made on the Stratford, the producer was foolish enough to offer a cash inducement to the owner of a line of washing so that she would remove it. In seconds, every single boat sported flapping garments – washed or otherwise. Today the flower people have gone – perhaps to Isis Lock or suburbia – and now holidaymakers can moor their boats at Lapworth. Which is what we did, early, because we were expecting friends to supper.

As evening drew in, a fluting bird note began. I listened, focusing the binoculars on some larch trees in the general direction of the song. Nothing. Curiosity took me along the towpath towards the next lock. The source of the trilling and piping turned out to be a caged cockatiel on the roof of a cruiser belonging to two of our former customers.

And so began the first hot, dry summer for many years although we did not know it then. Prepared as we were for all the adversities of English weather, two thirds of our clothes never emerged from the cupboard. The large umbrella we had bought to keep the steerer dry in long river reaches was ultimately used as a parasol to protect us from burning ultra-violet rays! Lucifer, in his black fur coat, lay motionless on the cool vinyl beneath the sofa, day after day.

But as we worked our way steadily down the flight, we revelled in the balmy weather, not expecting it to last more than a day or two. With their single gates and small paddles, the narrow locks emptied and filled slowly, giving us ample time to dream and gaze and (if you are like Maurice) recite chunks of Shakespeare. A sleepy adder curled around the ground paddle at lock 24 cut short a lengthy soliloquy.

"That's the second time we've seen a snake here!" he said in surprise. "Last time, Bruce found a water-snake – remember?" I nodded. It had been swimming in the lock until he coaxed it (how - I forget) out through the bottom gate to safety. Only then were we allowed to fill the lock and enter.

At Dick's Lane Wharf, we tied up alongside the barrel-roofed lock cottage to say hullo to Doug and Jane Smith. We sat in their sunlit garden to drink coffee while Jane took time off from painting canal-ware. Her studio was an old railway carriage, motionless in its final resting place. Their house is less peaceful than it used to be now that the M42 crosses the canal above lock 28.

It is believed that the limited scope of the canal builders led to the curious roof shape of these lock cottages. The labourers knew how to build tunnels and bridges, so what was more natural than to put a tunnel-top on a house? The cottage at Preston Bagot used to be of special interest. It was owned by a waterway enthusiast, Aubrey Wagstaffe, who modernised it with sensitivity. He kept a Visitor's Book on behalf of the local Canal Society and was always ready to have a chat about waterway affairs. Unhappily, he sold it. No doubt his heart grieves to see the gothic conversion it is now, with turrets and tinted one-way glazing in the patio doors!

Dick's Lane Wharf

Our overnight mooring lay above Lock 39, the only isolated one and aptly named The Odd Lock. It used to be accompanied by a lock cottage, long since demolished although rambler roses and peonies still struggle to survive in the relic of its garden. I raised the bottom paddle and glanced towards the Edstone aqueduct which carries the waterway across a stream, a road and a railway. A major engineering feature of the Stratford, its iron trough is 475 feet long and 175 years old.

As I watched, a party of walkers appeared on the far side of the aqueduct. They were led by a butch young woman who was striding manfully in our direction. By the time we were through the lock, many were on the aqueduct, hot foot in pursuit of their leader who ignored them. We crossed the aqueduct ourselves; calling greetings to her followers who were too out of breath to reply.

"Gosh!" I said, "what a pace!"

"Here are more," said Maurice as we came out from under Bridge 57. "These can't keep it up, obviously."

This lot were peeling off sweatshirts and pullovers as they scampered after each other. They grinned at us wryly. We came to another bend. Still more appeared, red-faced and walking at a more reasonable rate. After that, they turned up in threes and fours and getting slower with each successive group. Then the gaps between groups got longer; one or two people showing signs of real fatigue.

"That's the lot," said Maurice, as the last few stragglers limped away. But a quarter of a mile further on, we saw a man patiently waiting for his wife to catch him up. She smiled wanly as we cruised by. "That *must* be all."

I agreed. But lo – a good ten minutes later we came across a solitary lady of advanced years. She was carrying one shoe and tottering her lonely way after the others.

I had been hoping to sketch one of the split bridges which are a distinctive feature of the canal. There are only two types of original bridge on the southern section; brick arches spanning both canal and towpath are rated at 5 tons capacity; those spanning only the water are rated at 1 ton. The iron railings of the latter are flanked by red brick from which the iron decks are cantilevered in two halves. A one inch slot along the centre allowed the towing-rope to pass through without being unhitched from the horse.

Near Wilmcote, I saw an ideal bridge below a lock. Afternoon sun warmed the old brickwork and picked out the tracery of ironwork. Rosebay willowherb brightened the lush growth around the lock entrance. I have never seen such a motley conglomeration of timber as that which patched the flimsy bottom gate. The painting went well until the sun slipped suddenly behind tall trees, throwing deep shadows over the scene.

"That's that!" I said to Maurice. "I can finish it from memory at home."

Not only was our mooring too close to the lock for comfort, but a short pound is not a sensible place in which to spend the night, so we pushed on down through the rest of the Wilmcote flight to Stratford. The last bridge, carrying throngs of tourists, can be tricky. The underside slopes and appears to offer more headroom than it actually has. Also, the remains of the demolished towpath used to lurk beneath the surface on the right hand side and may do still. We had a narrow squeak once but this time negotiated it safely.

The canal had crept surreptitiously into Stratford behind faceless walls. Suddenly we emerged into the hurly-burly of Bancroft Gardens. The terminal basin was rimmed with boats in festival rig and surrounded by crowds of visitors. Amazingly, we found a vacant mooring almost at the feet of the stone bard.

"It looks like a rally," said I, and so it turned out be. We walked round the basin and found several familiar faces on board the other boats. Most of them had been there since Friday evening and it was now Sunday. There were a couple of canal society stands selling gifts, books (mine among them, I was gratified to observe), and giving information about the Stratford upon Avon Canal.

We walked across to the theatre to see if we could get cancellations for A Midsummer Night's Dream and found to our disappointment that the B.B.C. Symphony Orchestra was playing that night instead. The R.S.C. has Sundays off, apparently.

"What about tomorrow?" Maurice scanned the list of performances but The Dream alternated with Lear, which he cannot abide. Perhaps it is our own fault for not booking in advance but if you do, the pressure is on to be in a certain place at a specific time. Boating can be so unpredictable and theatre tickets are too expensive to waste.

Oddly enough, in spite of the mass of humanity and roar of vehicles which had greeted us, the night was fairly peaceful. The next morning, a short walk away from the tourist traps took us to shops selling more mundane goods where we topped up our supplies. Another vital purchase was a combined licence to cruise both the Upper and Lower Avon Navigations which are operated by charitable trusts.

This meant a death defying dash through the traffic on Clopton Bridge to Stratford Marine which is tucked into the peninsula on the other side. Inspired by the collection of chandlery, Maurice also bought a mooring rope which the proprietor offered to splice. His wife was intrigued to learn that we had recently closed our shop and the four of us discussed at some length the pros and cons of running waterside businesses.

By then, the boats attending the rally were dispersing and we had to wait our turn to descend the wide barge-lock onto the River Avon. Not only the lock but the river seemed spacious after the narrow canal we had just left. We swept downstream past the Memorial Theatre, trying to avoid running down numerous skiffs whose occupants seemed oblivious of other river traffic. A pair of blue and yellow narrow boats was moored alongside the Recreation Ground at the temporary moorings. They advertised themselves as a shop which I thought was tough on Stratford Marine.

Then we arrived at Stratford New Lock which is situated opposite Holy Trinity Church. William Shakespeare lies buried in the chancel. I made brass rubbings there when I was a schoolgirl. There was some controversy about New Lock when it was built, I recall. A conventional lock would have been unable to withstand the ground pressures and so it had to be reinforced by rectangular steel girder frames. Certain factions objected to its appearance close to a building associated with Shakespeare and lobbied to prevent its erection. We visited the site when the project was under way and talked to David Hutchings about the problems he was having with the opposition. It was a cold, wet winter's day. He and his team from Winson Green Prison were working in a quagmire. His vision of the ugly metal structure being absorbed into its surroundings was difficult to share on that occasion. Now, painted a discreet green and surrounded by willows and other attractive trees, it is far from being the eyesore that was threatened and no worse than the Memorial Theatre itself. Close by stands a monument celebrating the reopening of the navigation in 1974. Maurice attended the ceremony, again performed by the Queen Mother, by car.

The throngs were left behind as we dropped down through the lock and then we were breaking new ground. Warwickshire Lad had been waiting fifteen years to cruise the Warwickshire Avon. The river rises at Welford on the border of Leicestershire and Northamptonshire and flows into the mighty Severn at Tewkesbury. Sadly, the Avon is one of the most polluted rivers in England. My school-friends and I often used to swim in its clear waters at Alveston. Now, the river has a dark, unhealthy greenness telling of nitrogen as well as unseen chemical waste. I have read of a town upstream which draws its drinking water out of the Avon *below* its own sewage outfall! Personally, I would not allow a dog to swim in the river today.

It is not easy to tie up at whim on many rivers and the Avon is no exception. Much of the land seemed privately owned and inhospitable. However, there were designated moorings at most locks. This did not automatically mean that we would find a space. We had been warned about this and planned to knock off each afternoon early enough to make sure of one. By Luddington, our stomachs were rumbling and all we wanted to do was pause for lunch. The only vacancy was half our length but the obliging crews of the boats on either side each shifted up enough for us to squeeze in between. That was the only time we had the least problem mooring in the whole of our trip downstream. We ate our salad in the mottled shadow of the willows between the lock and the weir stream which raced angrily over rocky outcrops. Three ladies were sketching the foaming water over which the wires of a canoe course were stretched. They were members of an art class doing their homework, they told me with enthusiasm. I looked at the subject they had chosen and decided that it was too difficult for me.

The thermometer crept up through the eighties day by day. By four o'clock on most afternoons we were more than ready to stop in the shade. This was not always possible. Some of the moorings were in blazing sun, in which case we went on to the next if we could. Shamefully, I have to admit that we were too hot or too idle to keep a log. I had even forgotten my diary.

Murky the water may be but the surroundings of the Avon are more picturesque than any other river we have cruised. Undulating, wooded countryside sprinkled with pretty hamlets and handsome houses flank the restored navigation. There was a superfluity of subjects to paint. The sun was high overhead when we arrived at E. & H. Billington Lock close by the hamlet of Barton. A group of mellow stone buildings roofed in lichen-covered slate and topped by an engaging crooked dovecote grabbed my eye.

"Oh – just look at that!" I said to Maurice as we looped on to one of the moorings. Unfortunately, the perfect view-point was extremely uncomfortable. I flattened the nettles and spread a rug over them to protect my ankles and Maurice rigged up the brolly to stop me getting sunstroke. I painted as fast as I could, sloshing water across the paper to compensate for speedy evaporation. An hour and a half later, with stinging legs and burnt arms, I had finished and we were on our way. There is a riverside path to the same place. It begins in the carpark at Bidford-on-Avon and ends at the Cottage of Content in Barton – a winter ramble I can recommend.

Most of the public moorings at Bidford were occupied but we were lucky enough to find a space almost at the beginning of the line and handy for one of several waterpoints. Refuse bins were plentiful too. At the top of the steep, grassy bank picnickers sat alongside their cars beneath the trees. Apart from one small cruiser, I had an uninterrupted view of the long pack-horse bridge of which no two arches are identical. The square tower of Bidford church rose from the willows beyond. Perching on a stool underneath the umbrella on the stern counter, I got out my paints for the second time that day. Sunlight glared on the warm stone face of the bridge; dazzling me with its reflection in the water. At dusk, musicians began to tune up and microphones were adjusted at an open-air bar opposite. We enjoyed the nostalgia of sixties hits muted by the width of the river.

The next morning we were dismayed to find that the newsagent did not stock the waterways magazines we used to sell. I tried to get him to mend his ways without success. Then we trod carefully down a mucky alley to Bidford Boats, anxious to learn more about their Dutch barge called Klementina. The place appeared to be deserted. I noticed Maurice looking longingly across at the barge as we cruised downstream. It was an imposing vessel.

"Hm," I murmured. "I reckon we could live on one of those quite happily. I'd love to see what it's like inside."

The guide book was packed with warnings about keeping to this or that channel for unexplained reasons. We meticulously followed the advice we were given but I observed that several other boats did not and came to no harm. I would not like to chance my luck after heavy rain when the current is strong, though. At George Billington Lock Maurice emptied the bucket into one of the rudimentary sani-disposals. They were efficient, vandal-resistant and fairly numerous. On the lock-side stood an unusual lock-keeper's hut called The

Offenham Light which looked like a mini-lighthouse. It was flood-proof.

"Good gracious!" I exclaimed, getting out my camera. "Does the water level really get that high?" England was in the grip of a drought by this time so the hut was unoccupied. Maurice obligingly nipped up the spiral staircase and posed for a photograph. During the weekend, the locks were manned by volunteers – some of whom were an asset and some who were not. Still, the motives of all of them were good, I am sure.

This was the last lock of the Upper Navigation although the actual boundary between the two authorities is level with the Bridge Inn at Offenham. Thus, Evesham Lock with its triangular lock cottage straddling the chamber – another of David Hutchings' controversial designs – was the first lock of the Lower Navigation. The lock-keeper was in residence and witnessed the mess I made of entering the chamber. I mistook the sluice gates on the right for the lock gates, realised the error too late and ended up impaled on the spit of land in between. There *were* locks where a mistake of that sort might have ended up in shooting an unguarded weir.

Not all official moorings were situated at lock approaches. The other sort are small quays, often in the middle of nowhere, which sometimes appeared unexpectedly. We rounded Craycombe Turn and saw one. There were two other boats there, with room for a couple more. You must not be shy on the Avon. With restricted mooring there is no alternative to spending the night cheek by jowl even if you prefer solitude. We were acquainted with the occupants of one, which had been at the rally in Bancroft Gardens, and chatted aimiably until madam said she had 'boatwork' to do. The others, whose children were swimming in the vile water, kept to themselves. I sketched a group of three pollarded willows on the far bank, light airs riffling their reflections, until Maurice brought me a refreshing sun-downer.

Fladbury Lock was our first on a day which promised to be another scorcher. We locked down with the Ambroses in the pride of their fleet of hired boats. All their craft are named after roses, some of which I have never seen mentioned in any gardening catalogue. Glancing back as we left the lock cut, I saw Fladbury Mill above the great weir. When Bruce was about eleven he stayed with a school friend whose family own the mill. He and his pals used to shoot the rapids and the weir in coracles

– those unstable round vessels of Welsh origin. I was glad not to have seen the weir until now!

We must have stocked up well in Stratford, because even at Pershore we did not need to stop for provisions although we considered it. But the first lot of moorings did not appeal to us so we pressed on through the lock. Threatened turbulence around the piers of the old bridge failed to materialise, probably due to the drought, and the second, short line of moorings was full. Pershore was left behind quickly.

Then we came to the most attractive reach of the Avon yet. Giant trees clothed the slopes on the left, sprinklers watered agricultural land on the right. I savoured a delicious moment of coolness as the arc of spray swept over us and the cabin roof steamed briefly. We were aiming for Comberton Quay which turned out to be even shorter than Craycombe Turn – room for only two boats and one was there already. Every available surface of the vessel was crammed with pots of petunias, begonias, fuchsias, marigolds, lobelia, sweet alyssum....and a comprehensive watering programme was being undertaken. We tied up next door in blistering heat. The sun scorched the tiny quay which was tucked into a fold of the steep, tree-covered hill behind it. Heaven knows what the thermometer would have read if we had had one on board.

Lucifer lay flat on the floor as if he were dead. Strangely enough, his fur felt cool. I closed the curtains and left him as much ventilation as possible. Then we sweated our way up the hill to find the farm to which some friends of ours from Birmingham days had moved. What bliss to relax with a cold lager in their shady garden for an hour or two and catch up on all our news. Although we had arrived unexpectedly, they pressed us to stay for supper. While we were there an itinerant greengrocer turned up on his regular round which was our good fortune. Finally, when the sun had burned its way below the horizon, Charles and Jill strolled down to Warwickshire Lad with us for coffee. Lucifer, I was relieved to find, had come to life and was his usual ravenous, affectionate self.

Gradually the boat cooled although no breeze stirred the sheltering trees round us. Silently, the river flowed. Every twenty minutes or so, a nearby sprinkler made its regular pass over the reeds, scattering drops with a whisper. Eventually, I was lulled to sleep in the airless cabin.

After a restless night, we woke early and wasted no time in getting going. The Avon meandered towards Eckington; past Nafford lock where there was a nature reserve on the adjoining island. The weir stream went off to the right of the island and another stream flowed through a sluice to the left of the lock. A swing bridge carrying the footpath actually straddled the chamber. I could not bring Warwickshire Lad in until Maurice had swung the bridge out of the way.

Shortly afterwards we negotiated the tightest turn yet, the Swan's Neck, where there was an uninviting small quay actually on the 180 degree bend. Meanwhile, Bredon Hill glowered down at us, first from one side and then from the other. We saw many swan families on that particular reach. Mama led the way in stately fashion followed by a row of cygnets, swimming naughtily out of line occasionally. Papa cruised in the rear, constantly on the look-out for danger.

An apparently insignificant stream called Bow Brook flows into the Avon above Strensham Lock. If you look at the Ordnance Survey, you will see that it gathers water from myriads of tributaries born in the West Midlands. Not only did the Avon become abruptly wider but the current speeded up noticeably. Its course straightened and seemed tedious by comparison with the upper reaches. A fishing match was in progress. Coach loads of participants were being disgorged onto the already crowded banks. In spite of the breadth of the river, oaths rained thickly on our heads as we slipped past.

It had been deceptively cool all morning. Moorings in Tewkesbury were obviously at a premium so we tied up among overhanging trees at the scruffy end of a pub garden. Dutifully, we gave them the benefit of our custom and planned a second visit to the bar after we had toured the town. New licensing laws meant that pubs could stay open all day. Not in Tewkesbury, as it turned out.

Pavements burned underneath my rubber soled shoes; shop fronts glittered; narrow streets overhung with Elizabethan half-timbering created funnels of dusty heat. The bank's cash dispenser swallowed my card. At a quaint restaurant, we perspired in uncomfortable mock-Tudor chairs for forty minutes before we were served. Lorries constantly thundered past the open door. Neither of us had any appetite left by the time the food arrived.

After lunch, we crossed the road to the abbey church which is as large as a cathedral. As we entered the west door, the cold atmosphere wrapped round me like a wet flannel.

"Heaven." I murmured. "Sheer heaven." I would have stayed longer in the chilly draught if Maurice had not insisted that I move. There was a thrumming of activity inside as a large team of young people under the auspices of Cathedral Camps beavered away; cleaning marble, polishing everything from rood-screen to pew, removing rust and painting iron-work. A strong smell of beeswax and turpentine pervaded the dank air. It was not restful but I was loth to go.

Leaving the church was like stepping into an oven. Keeping to the shady side of the street, we made our way back to Warwickshire Lad to find the pub closed and a stroppy note slapped on the cabin side with a demand for two pounds. Happily, there was no-one about to collect it otherwise there might have been an argument. Letting go the ropes, Maurice pushed the bow out into the current and we headed for the narrow navigation arch of King John's Bridge. On the right after that, a wooden jetty filled with waiting boats heralded the lock which would remove us from the River Avon onto Severn waters.

=18=

UPHILL & DOWN

There seemed to be a certain amount of disorganisation around Avon Lock. We approached slowly and I managed to jump onto the end of the jetty and persuade the owner of the next boat to move it along a bit, which he did reluctantly. Several craft were queueing on either side of the entrance plus one cruiser standing off in midstream. At first glance, the chamber appeared to be empty with bottom gates open and no sign of a boat coming in. A notice-board on the side of the lock-house instructed waiting skippers to switch off engines. Maurice did so. I inquired of our neighbour what was going on but he had no idea. A sun-tanned fellow dressed only in shiny swimming trunks appeared from the lower level and started bossing everyone about, including me.

"Move back, darlin'," he ordered, which made me bristle. We were right at the end of the jetty – any further and I would have fallen off! "Back! Back!" he repeated with such vigour that we loosed the ropes and I hung on with the long shaft to a bent bit of scaffolding. Large rocks scraped the hull threateningly. The next-door boat was moved into our space.

After an age, a tiny cruiser mounted the lock and was nursed out by Satin Trunks who moored it to the jetty. We eventually learnt that its engine had failed on the Old Avon, the short link between the lock and the Severn. As the boat was recently purchased in Tewkesbury, the lock-keeper was helping its new owner return it to the vendor. This was magnanimous of him and we would have understood perfectly had we known that he actually *was* the lock-keeper and not just a scantily dressed busybody.

As the lock was mechanised, we needed to do nothing more than loop the ropes round bollards on the lock-side and pay them out as the level fell. Then we were on our way, thankful to leave the commotion behind. The chart warned us of a shoal projecting from the north bank at the junction of the two rivers and we kept well clear. It is a temptation to cut the corner, which one of the boats sharing our lock did and ran aground behind us. The other had previously caught the mud bank opposite the Town Quay and slewed to a sluggish stop. For once, our slavish adherence to the navigational notes paid off.

Feeling unashamedly smug, we cruised out into the main river and headed straight upstream for Telford's Mythe Bridge.

The river Severn rises on the north-eastern slopes of Plynlimon in the Cambrian Mountains and flows by a tortuous route into the Bristol Channel. Its two hundred and twenty miles from source to sea make it the longest river in Britain and it has been one of the principal navigations of England since medieval times. Spring tides flow upriver as far as Tewkesbury, above which the river is non-tidal. Diglis lock in Worcester links the Severn to the Worcester & Birmingham Canal. Twelve and a half miles upstream from there is Stourport and the junction with the Staffs & Worcester Canal. Barely a few hundred yards further on you come to the official limit of navigation at the present time.

Drought conditions prevailing in Wales were evident from the level of the Severn. Much of its banks are supported by huge slabs of granite which are normally two-thirds submerged. Now, they stood proud of water which lapped grey beaches of drying mud. Bridge footings were exposed and the figure nought on flood markers stood high and dry. Warwickshire Lad made fair progress upstream against a slack current; keeping well away from hazardous shallows near the banks, especially on bends. But the river is wide and there was plenty of room for other, faster, boats to overtake and leave us bobbing about in their wake.

The view was limited. Well wooded high banks obscured the countryside. At least we created our own cooling breeze out in the middle of the river.

The sun was sinking when we reached Upton upon Severn. There were temporary moorings on the bank nearest the town. Wide-beam cruisers of the type commonly called 'bath tub' occupied them all. We cast about without success, even trying an unfriendly block of concrete almost underneath the bridge.

"I don't fancy the thought of someone dropping a brick on our roof from up there," Maurice said, eyeing a couple of lads who were looking over the parapet at us. "Let's go into the marina instead. We need water, anyway."

It was baking hot against the floating jetty but we could not face going on any further. The next public moorings would be at Kempsey, seven miles away, and they would probably be full by now anyway. Our plan for the morrow was to aim for a spot on the eastern bank directly opposite the site of the battle of Worcester which took place in 1651. It is on a bend just after the confluence of the Teme and the Severn. You may be wondering why? The answer is that by happy chance my sister Cassie and her husband live in an enviable house high up on the river bank. Their extensive garden is terraced down to the towpath which also belongs to them. Unfortunately, the bank has been damaged by the breaking wash of large cruisers and trip boats. To moor there is impossible. However, their neighbours' bank was not in quite such a sorry state and they also have a small wooden jetty which they had given us permission to use. We thought there might be a chance of success there in the morning – but preferably not at dusk.

After a refreshing beer at Ye Olde Anchor Inn, we strolled back across Upton Bridge to the marina and made use of their payphone. Cassie and Patrick drove out to see us and we spent a jolly evening consuming Pat's homemade wine and making plans for the next day.

"How on earth can we tell from the river which garden belongs to Terry and Liz?" I asked.

"Look out for our trees," advised my sister."

"I'll fix a burgee to one near the jetty," said Pat when they were leaving for home. "What time d'you reckon?"

We thought it would take about three hours to cover the ten miles from Upton but it was longer. The sun beat mercilessly down on us as we ploughed upstream. We took turns to cower beneath the umbrella but the glittering light reflected off the water was almost as painful as the glare from the sky. A puff of air briefly felt in an open reach might have come straight from the Sahara.

At last I glimpsed the tops of some cypresses which I recognised. At the same moment Maurice spied the burgee fluttering from a willow and we turned in towards one of a number of jetties in the locality. Then Pat appeared, having been watching the river through binoculars from the balcony. With difficulty, because the jetty was intended for fishing not mooring, he and Maurice made Warwickshire Lad secure. Luckily, overhanging willows created a small amount of dappled shade on the roof. Lucifer was playing dead again, so we left him in peace and climbed up the iron ladder through the nettles to the crumbling towpath.

It was fresher on the top lawn in front of the house. The day was spent lolling in the shade followed by a barbecue in the evening. Now and again, I descended to the hot river bank to check on Lucifer. At bedtime, we negotiated the steep, twisting path and the treacherous ladder by torchlight.

Breakfast, cooked by Patrick and eaten on the terrace preceded our departure. Either the current or a drop in water level had grounded the boat firmly and I waded into the tepid shallows to help push off. Then we were away; my sister and brother-in-law waving from the tiny jetty until the willows screened them from view.

Leaving the Severn turned out to be more of a brouhaha than entering it. Approaching the pair of Diglis locks, we observed that the traffic light was red so we turned in towards the right-hand side of the lock approach to make fast and wait. Unfortunately, the lock-keeper opened the sluices seconds before we made it. The tremendous surge of water sucked the boat into the mouth of the lock where we totally lost control. Crash after crash occurred as the boat was hurled from one side of unforgiving stone to the other. It was terrifying but no actual harm was done. As soon as the great lock was empty, normality returned. The gates purred open and a cluster of cruisers emerged. Maurice heaved himself up onto the towpath and with quietening heart I drove Warwickshire Lad into the chamber, trying to look as if I had never lost command. I slung the ropes up to Maurice, high on the lock-side. The lock-keeper reckoned another boat was on the way so we waited patiently for ten minutes until it arrived.

There was plenty of turbulence when the lock filled. Even though Maurice had roped on securely, the boat swung about. The lock seemed to fill faster than we could take up the slack.

Worcester Cathedral came into view as we approached the locks which lead from the Severn into the two Diglis basins and the Worcester & Birmingham Canal. There were all sorts of boats, waiting at the jetty so we drew in behind the last one. The lock, operated under the supervision of the keeper, accommodated us all and we passed through smoothly. At the second lock he was not to be seen. Up zoomed the paddles – large ones. In surged the water.

Warwickshire Lad, being steel, was nearest the top gate. Behind me lay a large fibreglass cruiser with an inboard motor. At the rear sat a small cruiser with an outboard. I think the middle man was probably responsible for drawing the paddles. We were all roped on, of course. The force of the water was such that neither the ropes nor the engine in full forward throttle could stop our boat from being forced astern. Large Cruiser yelled at me not to bend his chrome pulpit-rail and Small Cruiser had hysterics about his outboard. I was doing my best. The palms of my hands were raw by the time Maurice got at the paddles and half lowered them. By then, Large Cruiser looked a bit sheepish but he concealed this by denigrating narrow boats and extolling the virtues of a zed-drive – whatever that may be.

Thankfully, none of the Upton registered boats went on further than the Commandery. I guess it was just a Sunday outing and this was their limit of navigation. By lock number five we realised that we had been spoilt by the comparative depth of the rivers. There was an obvious shortage of water in the canal. A boat moored below the lock jutted far out at the stern. Its hirer related a garbled tale of broken paddles or gates, he was not sure which.

"It looks O.K. to me," I announced, having examined it. The lock was empty and the other people did not want to go through so we did. Ahead of us, I could see at least one boat waiting for the next lock. The pound looked low. "We'd better wait here," I added, "until they've gone up."

After twenty minutes a boat came down. The crew said that a boat was stuck in the pound above but someone was letting water down from the top. The top of where, I wondered? They entered the lock we had just left and we set off for the next, grinding along the bottom. We were second in the queue so decided to stand off near the centre of the channel until we could go straight in. But the boat coming out could not get past us. Our two vessels embraced at length. Meanwhile, the boat in front slithered into the lock. I watched it rise up and leave. One more lock full of water should see us clear, I anticipated. Then the horrible truth dawned. Boats were still coming up behind us! One, two, then a third. Our soul-mate was forcibly dragged away by its hefty crew of young men who promised to stop anyone filling the lock below until we were free. Two of them obligingly stayed to help Maurice bow-haul us forward. The hull scraped sickeningly across the stones and bounced over the cill into the lock. I prayed that the next pound would be no worse.

It was much the same and so was the one after that. The outskirts of Worcester were behind us before things improved at all. If we had been able to turn round at the start of the fiasco, I guess we would have gone back to the Severn and on to Stourport. I wondered whether the lock-keeper at Diglis knew what was happening up above him, and if he did, why he had not warned everybody. We shall never know.

There are fifty-six narrow locks between Diglis basin in the centre of Worcester and King's Norton Junction in Birmingham's suburbs. It took almost the whole of that day to do fourteen of them. Knowing that there was a popular pub at Dunhampstead and expecting the moorings there to be crowded, we stopped well short at Oddingly. The pity of it was that a pleasant rural canal should be spoilt by the battle to get uphill.

But the situation improved. Traffic thinned for some reason and the water marginally deepened. Tardebigge's flight of thirty was merely plain hard work which was to be expected. I began to appreciate the rolling countryside and summoned up the energy to clamber up the embankment to look at the reservoir. It was pitifully low.

There was only one lock between us and the summit by the time we knocked off in the long pound where a level towpath and stone piling offered a good overnight mooring. The evening was cool and fresh. I assure you we slept well that night!

A sparkling morning greeted us. I felt a vitality probably brought about by the height we had gained on the enervating river valley. Tardebigge Top Lock was a deep one and raised us the last fourteen feet to the Midlands plateau. We tied up on the towpath side behind another boat. Maurice went off to search in vain for fresh milk while I sketched the intriguing roof shapes of the British Waterways Maintenance Yard opposite. Then there was an interminable wait for our turn at the water point. The thin trickle from the tap when we finally got hold of it explained why.

Tardebigge Tunnel; Shortwood Tunnel; Alvechurch. We scampered down the hill to the shops and just caught them before they shut for lunch. Then a long drag back to the boat fully laden. A fresh wind blew across Lower Bittell Reservoir and tempted us to moor there. We battled with the breeze until a small, scruffy cruiser hove in sight. It was yawing uncontrollably, the cove at the helm giving forth a discordant song. He scraped by without, apparently, seeing us at all. By then, the wind had taken us past the only possible mooring.

"Forget it," said Maurice. I glanced back at the cruiser, which was heading full pelt for some reeds, and agreed that it might be wise. Hopwood used to be a tolerable place to spend the night but a foul smell forced us on to the next bridge. The bank was overgrown with spindly willows but there was a gap into which he edged the boat. A mat of duck-weed gradually enclosed the hull and spread across the canal. The floating vegetation supported a coca cola can. I stared, fascinated, as it inched past with the flow of water down distant Tardebigge. By morning, weed and can had disappeared.

King's Norton Tunnel cuts through Wast Hills; leaving Worcestershire behind somewhere in the middle and entering Warwickshire. I dislike tunnels and it is my second least favourite – Harecastle being the first. Blisworth Tunnel is longer but King's Norton is more oppressive. Although it is technically possible to see both ends at the same time, thick mist in the centre usually blots out the view. We were fairly new to boating when it was closed for repair. I shudder to remember the report we read at the time. Contractors were brought in. There were no records of the original engineering work which took place at the turn of the eighteenth century. The tunnel had been drained and work was progressing on the roof. Above the team, a shaft which had served to expel the spoil had been filled with rubble. The whole lot collapsed, pressing two men into a puddle. They drowned.

I was glad to emerge into the cutting at the northern end and aim for the sunlight slanting across the Green from King's Norton Junction where the Stratford upon Avon Canal goes off to the west. This is a place we know well. When we belonged to the Birmingham Canal Navigation Society some twelve years ago, one of our commitments was to walk a stretch of the B.C.N. every fortnight and report our findings. We checked water level and towpath condition; noting instances of fly-tipping, vandalism and so on. Our beat was from King's Norton Junction to Selly Oak station. It made a pleasant and useful Sunday morning stroll.

But now we turned right at the junction house, which was still surrounded by semi-vintage cars in various stages of decay. Then we halted by the blue brick coping and so far from the bank that the gangplank would not reach. The summit level must have been twelve inches off but I wanted to sketch the famous guillotine stop-lock. Tying up was Maurice's headache. I whipped out paper and paints as the sky darkened.

the famous guillotine stop-lock

The heat wave was over. Before my painting was completed, rain had begun. The air grew chill and a brisk wind got up and rattled the dehydrated leaves high above the lock.

"Another unfinished picture," I said ruefully; glad there had been time to capture the bow of a narrow boat under the nearer wooden guillotine. Only the reflections were lacking.

Once we had passed through a little swing bridge, the Birmingham conurbation skulked behind dense woodland. Brandwood tunnel hides itself in a leafy cutting which was starting to drip long-awaited rain. The heavy shower was scarcely enough to settle the dust and stopped as we emerged into the countryside round Earlswood. Oops! A careless young tractor driver was sitting dolefully on his half-submerged vehicle. He shook his fist as we altered course to avoid him and my camera shutter clicked. And then we were at Hockley Heath, where Maurice's parents used to live. We would have paused to have a beer for old times' sake but the wooden jetty had mostly been demolished and The Wharf appeared not to welcome boaters anymore. This seemed at odds with the extensive towpath improvements between the adjacent road bridge and the next, freshly painted lift bridge.

Lapworth Top Lock is numbered two, to take account of the stop-lock way back. We had a flight of nineteen to get us back onto the Grand Union at Kingswood Junction where our circuit of the Avon Ring began. A daunting task, you may think but I have always considered it a delight. The narrow locks are well spaced at first to get you into the swing; gathering momentum as you go. Thankfully, it was cooler than a week before. The scenery cannot be faulted and there are some widened intervening pounds alive with mallard parents and their offspring. At a sharp bend between locks seven and eight, there was a hold-up caused by a gaggle of boats, one of which was aground on a sneaky mud bank which never fails to catch a victim. Maurice hammered in one spike to which he looped both our ropes and we took the opportunity to have a late lunch.

By the time the way ahead was clear, most of the water had gone too. We had a job to get off the mud ourselves and into the lock. There were no more problems until we reached the basin at Kingswood which looked like an estuary when the tide is out. Lock twenty was full and unoccupied. Maurice jumped onto the bank and ran over the split bridge to open the gate. I steered a straight course between the two locks and got there safely.

Within ten minutes we were back on the Grand Union and heading south-east. It was raining again. I was soaked by the time White Bridge appeared and I pulled into the side.

"I'll put the canopy on," Maurice said for the first time since we left home. It was stiff and unyielding; turning slimy as soon as it got wet. I noticed a couple of splits in the canvas where it rubbed against the cratch.

"We need a new canopy," I pointed out. Maurice grunted. "There's a chap who makes them to measure at Buckby," I added temptingly. "At least – sometimes he's at Buckby."

"Terry Clapham," he replied. "Has a pair of boats – Seamus and Ely – one's his workshop."

"You knew?"

He nodded. "I've already talked to him about it. He'll give us a price next time he's our way."

It was lucky Maurice fixed it up then, because after our canopy was finished, Terry said he was thinking of selling up.

"What are you going to do?" I asked.

"Move to France," he said. "The canals there are much like they used to be here twenty years ago. Miles and miles of them – no crowds."

I sneaked a look at Maurice whose blue eyes were bright with interest. Long after Terry's pair of boats had descended Buckby locks we were talking about what he had told us.. Maurice found a copy of Imray's Map of the Inland Waterways of France and opened it out.

"Just look at that!" He traced his finger across the map. A network of navigable rivers and canals spread from the Netherlands to the Mediterranean, enmeshing, not only France but Germany and Belgium as well. "A vast area of waterways and we haven't even tried it."

"We took a trip on a *Bateau Mouche* in Paris on our honeymoon," I reminded him. "Perhaps it was an omen."

He smiled. "Maybe. Let's see what else we can discover." The more we read, the keener our enthusiasm grew. Eventually, we made our plans thus: sell up, store our stuff, buy a barge and take off for the waterways of Western Europe for as long as it takes.

And that promises to be another story.

THE AUTHOR

Shirley Ginger was born into an artistic family in Darlington, County Durham. She married an officer in the Royal Warwickshire Regiment when she was barely twenty and spent the first twelve years of married life globe-trotting from one army posting to another. When her husband finally left the service they settled in Birmingham where she had previously studied art. While their two children were growing up she ran her own small business there and achieved an Open University B.A. Ten years ago they escaped from the rat race to a waterside small-holding in the Shires where she wrote 'Lock, Stock & Barrel' followed by the perennial best seller 'Simple Steps to Roses & Castles', a beginner's guide to the technique of narrow boat painting. 'Fen Tigers was the first in a series of Travers and Marshall waterways mysteries. Now in her fourth book, we have 'A Bit More Boating' to round off the story of life at Buckby Wharf.